Judson Cornwall states, "Perhaps the greatest uniqueness of this book on togetherness is that it emphasizes that getting together as Christians is totally dependent upon our getting together with Christ Jesus as individuals. It is our distinctive differences that make us so valuable one to another, but only a common life can unite such diversity. Our union with Christ makes possible our unity one with another."

In *Let Us Get Together*, Judson Cornwall teaches all Christians, old and new, to enjoy fully a more rewarding relationship with God and a richer fellowship with other believers.

Let Us Get Together

Judson Cornwall, Th.D.

Fleming H. Revell Company
Old Tappan, New Jersey

Library of Congress Cataloging in Publication Data

Cornwall, Judson.
  Let us get together.

  1. Christian union. 2. Christian life—
1960–   . I. Title.
BX8.2.C63 1983   262'.0011   82–16630
ISBN 0–8007–5103–5

TO Emalene Shepherd,
who is not only a dedicated instructor in the art of writing
but is gifted with the ministry of encouragement. Without
her consistent encouragement and concern my first book
might very well have been my last. To you, Sis Shepherd, I
dedicate book number twelve.

Contents

Let Us Get Together

Ephesians 1–4

Acknowledgments

Wives of writers need to be saints just to preserve their sanity. My wife has become accustomed to my slipping to my typewriter in the middle of the night to put on paper what was stirring in my mind amidst sleepless meditation. Because I travel so widely, writing consumes a large block of my time when I am home. Surely if God intends to distribute any awards for writing books, my wife, Eleanor Cornwall, will be among the honorees.

Another of those who labor behind the scenes on every book is my secretary, Cheryl Tipon, who is not only skilled in typing but equally skilled in grammar, punctuation, and spelling. I deeply appreciate the many hours of loving labor that she has invested in this book.

Preface

Are any of us unaware of the plea of Jesus in His high priestly prayer, "That they all may be one; as thou, Father, art in me, and I in thee, that they also may be one in us: that the world may believe that thou hast sent me" (John 17:21)? It has been preached and written about very widely in the past ten years.

I've participated in regional conventions that were billed as John 17:21 conventions. I have spent hours on panels discussing this verse, and I have written multiple pages of notes of what others have had to say about our becoming one, like Jesus and His Father. The need for true Christians to be united is self-evident, but the nature of how it can be done remains hidden. In a recent conference in Canada an immigrant from Holland told me that during World War II the churches and clergy of that oppressed nation were united beyond belief, but that after the war was over they became segmented and went their separate ways until today, by his observation, the divisions are greater than before the war began. Is it possible that only *need* can cause us to get together?

Or is it possible that the true Church is together in God's sight far more than we realize? Could it be that in spite of our rhetoric to the contrary, we are still thinking of organizational uniformity when we use the word *unity?*

I was scheduled to speak at a conference in a community that experienced severe division among the Christians several years ago. This conference was an attempt to unite these factions in fellowship with each other, in spite of their differences in organizational views. The conference directors sent me several letters explaining the weight of the issue and reminding me that the success or failure of the conference pretty well rested on my shoulders. "It is imperative," they wrote, "that you have the mind of the Lord in your preaching."

Two days before the conference I was still unsure of what to share. Our congregation here at Fountain Gate meets every Tuesday evening for prayer and worship, and since I was home for a few days, I joined them. I had hardly begun to pray when a hand pressed on my shoulder and our pastor said, "I'm sorry to interrupt your praying, Judson, but I feel that the Lord wants me to ask you if you have ever considered the word *together* as it is used in the book of Ephesians?"

Without getting off my knees, I looked up and merely said, "No, I don't believe that I have."

"Well I feel that you should," she told me in a gentle and almost apologetic way.

"I'll do so when I have some time," I replied almost impatiently.

"But, Judson," she continued, "I feel that the Lord wants you to share this with the conference to which you are going."

"Not a chance," I declared. "The conference begins Thursday. There isn't enough time to develop new material now. Besides, you know how negative my feelings are about taking new material to a convention. I always want to preach it here first where you and the staff can judge its content and help me keep it balanced and consistent with the Word."

"I know," she said. "I'm not trying to push you; I'm only obeying God by telling you what I felt He was saying."

I returned to prayer and pushed the incident to the back of my mind, but about three o'clock in the morning I awakened with the word *together* echoing in the corridors of my mind. I dressed and went to my study to begin researching. By the time I caught my plane on Thursday, the background for this book was in outline form. I presented it during the conference, and God did a mighty healing among the people. While flying directly from that conference on the East Coast to one on the West Coast, I reviewed my notes since the preaching was still fresh in my mind. As I added a thought here and there, the Spirit spoke in my heart and said, "There's a book there if you are willing to write it."

I expanded the outline, wrote the first chapter, and sent it to Fleming Revell. Their response was, "Write it! We believe it will bless the Body of Christ."

Now the book is a reality. I can only hope that it is as liberating and inspirational to you who read it as it was to me as I spent months writing it. I can't shake the conviction that God is answering Christ's prayer right in our lifetime.

Let Us Get Together

Section I

God's Purpose for Getting Us Together

Having made known unto us the mystery of his will, according to his good pleasure which he hath purposed in himself: that in the dispensation of the fulness of times he might gather together in one all things in Christ, both which are in heaven, and which are on earth; even in him.

Ephesians 1:9,10

1

Man's Purpose for Getting Together

God is a good God! The Scriptures declare it (*see* Psalms 100:5), the saints have testified to it (*see* Psalms 34:8), and redeemed sinners have experienced it. God is not merely good in disposition; He is inherently good. That is His nature.

It stands to reason, then, that everything that God does will be good, for God cannot violate His own nature. Yet God Himself admitted that one thing He did was not good. Having viewed His work of creation step by step, ". . . the Lord saw that it was good" (Genesis 1:4,10,12,18,21,25) until He reviewed the apex of all creation—man—at which point we read, ". . . the Lord God said, It is *not good* that the man should be alone . . ." (Genesis 2:18, italics added). Creating Adam as a single entity was seen as "not good," so God redid this one act of creation and segmented Adam into two complete persons called Adam and Eve.

Aloneness is not good. God says so, and human experience cries the loud "Amen!" Aloneness is hellish. Just ask any prisoner in solitary confinement. Aloneness is emptiness and heartache, as any widow can attest. The aged who live alone will tell you that aloneness can be terrifying, while the teenager might call it depressing. The traveling man in his single motel room will quickly admit to being lonely, and many divorced individuals have discovered that the pain of being alone is worse than the pain they had experienced in their marriage.

Man's Need to Get Together

"It is not good that the man should be alone" was not a commandment of God; it was an observation. Man was created a social creature who cannot violate his inherent nature without paying a penalty, and aloneness carries a price tag so high that few can afford it, as any psychiatrist will affirm.

When faced with a solitary situation, most Americans seek a substitute companion in a pet, television, radio, a book, or in spectator sports. Even early-morning joggers are frequently seen carrying blaring portable radios to break the feeling of aloneness. It is probable that most of the bars in America would go out of business if loneliness were banished from the lives of all her citizens. But no act of Congress, no pleasure, no amount of self-discipline can remove loneliness from the life of a solitary individual. He may learn to live with it, and he may even redirect that feeling into creative channels, but he will not abolish the empty feeling of being alone.

For over a decade now my ministry has called for extensive travel throughout the world. Although I am usually surrounded by people from the moment I leave home until I return again, I have learned by experience how lonely one can be in a crowd. There is no togetherness in idle chatter or mere social communication. Eating in a crowded dining room is not fellowship if I am seated at a table by myself, nor is speaking to large audiences socially fulfilling, because of the distance set between the speaker and the listeners.

The motel may have 200 filled rooms, but the moment the door to my room closes, I am very much alone. Of course I have adjusted and adapted to it, but I cannot honestly say that I am comfortable with it, and among my greatest joys in life is coming back to my wife and home.

God did not make any of us to live alone. He tried that in the beginning and declared that it was not good for the man to dwell alone. All of us can handle isolation for a brief period of time, especially if we know approximately when it will end, but an open-ended prospect of living separated from anyone who cares for us and shares life with us is a shattering experience. Aloneness can so fragment a person that it has become one of the most powerful tools used in brainwashing.

Man is incapable of complete independence because God made him a dependent creature. Man was created with an inherent need for fellowship with God and with his fellowman, but sin produced an artificial sense of independence. Isaiah summarized it by saying, "All we like sheep have gone astray: *we have turned every one to his own way;* and the Lord hath laid on him the iniquity of us all" (Isaiah 53:6, italics added). Sin caused man to break fellowship with God and with others. The attraction of sin was to ". . . be as gods . . ." (Genesis 3:5) rather than to remain dependent upon God.

Sin placed the "rights" of man above the sovereignty of God and the creature defied the Creator, thereby isolating himself from intimate relationship with God. The result was a horrible aloneness. Cut off from fellowship with God, removed from intimate association with the angels, and forever expelled from Eden's garden, Adam and Eve had only each other. If they lost this togetherness, they faced the lonesomeness Cain experienced after he slew his brother, Abel, in a fit of anger. This murder merely reinforced the magnitude of man's need to unite, for once again Adam and Eve were reduced to having only each other; they were cut off from God and cut off from their two sons.

Man's Getting Together With Man

The penalty of separation was so great that men and women voluntarily submerged their independence in order to blend their lives with one another—first in marriage, next in families, and eventually in communities. Men were learning that survival demanded togetherness, even though some of their motives and goals were far below ideal, just as is common among Christians in the Church today. As a matter of fact, my thirty years of pastoring have convinced me that it is easier to unite people out of selfish and improper motives than through divine and pure purposes. The human heart still wants to cling to something short of God.

There is a selfishness in the human nature that cannot be ignored. "What's in it for me" is a powerful motivation in all of us. Furthermore, there is a strong pride factor to be dealt with in all of our lives. Appealing to these strong drives can motivate most people into action far more rapidly than appealing to their Christian love, their sense of obligation, or their obvious responsibility. If these fail, we can, of course, always project deep guilt feelings and seek to settle this sense of guilt by action.

Babel—Genesis 11:1-9

The building of the tower of Babel is a prime example of united action out of wrong motivations. Perhaps never since the flood had men so totally united themselves in a common endeavor as in this building program. Finding a commodious plain in the land of Shinar, they built a city, and then they ambitiously proposed to build a memorial tower whose top would reach unto heaven (*see* Genesis 11:4). Lacking stone and mortar in this rich agricultural plain, they dug clay, formed and baked bricks, and used pitch for their mortar. It took united effort, and they must have expended limitless energy over a long period of time to fulfill such lofty ambitions.

Fundamentally these descendants of Noah wanted mutual protection, continuing unity, and unrestricted access to God, and they wanted to do it "their way." In the covenant of the rainbow God had pledged that He would never again destroy the earth by flooding. Furthermore, by the blood covenant of sacrifice He had made Himself accessible to all the inhabitants of the earth, and as long as they were worshipers of God, there would be a continuing basis for togetherness.

But God's methods and provisions almost always seem too abstract and simplistic to men. Unity in Christ because of substitutionary sacrifice has always been a difficult concept for men to embrace because it does not call for action on the part of the one being united. We don't feel comfortable being saved by grace alone; we consistently want it to be grace plus something. For these inhabitants of Shinar it was "saved by grace through faith" *plus* the tower of Babel. They could not be content to merely accept God's action; they united in an action of their own that would enable them to produce an access to God that could also become a fortress of protection to them. No matter how great the cost, they would rather build a stairway to heaven than build an

altar unto God. They judged their religious works superior
to God's righteous ways. Their works were difficult and de-
fiant and called for sacrifice and great unity, as most religious works do, but they did not produce the intended effect.

As a matter of fact, their self-serving program of unifica-
tion actually became the cause of their separation. Not only
did they fail to meet God at the top of their tower, they
failed to maintain a unity among themselves since God confused their language, thereby separating them perpetually—
for inability to communicate is ultimate separation. Their
goal of being united was commendable, but their method of
achieving that goal was controvertible because their motivation was rooted in contrivance rather than in acceptance of
God's plan.

If people could only learn from history, they would be
spared much heartache and failure, but mankind seems to
have learned very little from the history books; we go right
on making the same mistakes preceding generations have
made. Most attempts at getting together produce ambitious
programs that unite people in a common activity but fail to
unite them in God. Ambitious building programs have
united great groups of church members for a season, but differences of opinion or completion of the project often dis-
perse the very ones who united in the project.

Church history records that in many generations God has
sovereignly visited His people in a wave of revival that drew
men unto Himself in a vital way. In an effort to preserve this
unity of God and man there usually followed the development of an organization for the perpetuation of the truth
that was revealed during the divine visitation. Before long,
however, more energy was expended in building that orga-

nization than in maintaining a vital relationship with God, and a tower of Babel began to rise from the plain of God's visitation. Visitors to our nation are often amazed and confused at the number of such religious "towers" that have been constructed here. We have the "Methodist tower," the "Baptist tower," the "Lutheran tower," the "Pentecostal tower," and so forth.

Inasmuch as they "speak different languages" and seem unable to communicate with one another, it is much like the tower of Babel where man's language was originally confounded. All the energies to unite men religiously end up in separating them ultimately, for the program usually overwhelms the purpose.

It is not that we are unwilling to unite, but that we're far more inclined to unite in a common action than in a common acceptance of the work of Christ; and usually this form of uniting is rooted in selfish goals while motivated by impure and improper intentions. We're anxious to build a name or a kingdom for ourselves, but rarely are we equally anxious to unite unto Christ's name or come together for the enlarging of His kingdom. From Babel until now religious men have been willing to unite for the purpose of reaching God through good works, but their unity is short-lived, and their purposes fall short of accomplishment.

David's Ragged Army—1 Samuel 22:1,2

David was one of God's great saints who quickly learned how dangerous it was to be alone. The heroism that catapulted him into both the public eye and Saul's household through marriage soon became the occasion for envy and jealousy in the king, and David had to flee for his life, hiding in Adullam's cave. David's brothers and other relatives soon joined him because the rage of Saul was unbearable, and they feared for their lives. Although these brothers had always mocked and slighted David, they now demanded his protection. Furthermore, about 400 men who were in trouble with the king, deeply in debt, or merely discontented, gathered themselves to David and offered to serve as his army.

Surely David had enough troubles of his own without having to become the protector and provider for a family who had rejected him and for outlaws and political fugitives whose loyalty to him was certainly suspect, but David needed them equally as much as they needed him. Although it was not a love affair that brought them together, they had a common enemy to face, and they knew that they could withstand Saul's army better together than separately. It was the common foe that became the common denominator among them. They were united by fear and self-protection.

It is interesting that throughout the pages of church history mutual defense against a common enemy has often become a uniting force. When persecution threatened to destroy the Church, there was little separatism among the Christians. Doctrinal differences were set aside as they united in mutual defense. We have just come through a season where many were united in what I lightly refer to as "demon chasers united." What unity there was among those who were exercising their authority to cast out demons.

Even more current is the uniting of forces in what is being called the Moral Majority, seeking to bring morality back to America through the legislative process. Reading the list of speakers at many of these rallies reveals a strange mixture of doctrine, practice, ideologies, and faith. Under different circumstances these gentlemen might very well be attacking one another, but for the sake of a common enemy they have united in both mutual defense and mutual offense. How true that "war makes strange bedfellows."

It is not my purpose to make light of such unions, for David made it work for him most successfully. He welded his ragged group of malcontents into a most victorious army, and most of these men remained with David as his "mighty men" when the kingdom was finally given to God's anointed. But I would like to point out that partners in war do not necessarily become partners in peace. During World War II Russia and America stood together against Germany, but that wartime ally has been our most consistent enemy ever since the armistice was signed. Common defense is a uniting force only as long as we face a common enemy; it seldom continues long in a period of peace.

When Christians are welded together in a mutual defense pact, they usually become militant in attitude and combative in disposition. Since it is a common fear and hate that forms the uniting bond, their attention must constantly be directed to the enemy. Some groups speak far more of the devil than they do of God, while others build their congregations by stirring up emotions against other denominations or what they define as "sects." Militant songs and sermons may blend emotions, but unless those emotions are carefully directed, they are often used for infighting. When the common enemy flees, people often turn one against the other in a form of self-destruction that is fearsome.

God seeks to unite men in the bonds of love, while man takes the shortcut and unites men through fear and hate. The way of God produces eternal results, while man's way is temporary and often very destructive to the very ones who seek self-protection in their getting together.

Absalom—2 Samuel 15

Still another example of man's getting together with man in purposes far beneath God's high intentions is seen in David's son Absalom. In resentment at being separated from his father because he had avenged the rape of his sister, Absalom became a shrewd and dangerous politician. Daily he met people in the gates and listened to their grievances and problems. His consistent answer was, "Things would be far different if I were the king." Little by little he drew the hearts of the people to himself until he had amassed enough followers to insurrect against his father in open civil war. But for the intervention of God in Absalom's untimely death in battle, he might very well have succeeded.

Whenever there is a generous move of God's Spirit among His people, we can expect to see an Absalom or two sitting in the gates preaching their doctrine of "come out from among them, and join me!" There have always been leaders who prey upon the weaknesses of others to build their own kingdoms. They locate a point of discontent and blow it out of proportion, suggesting that their leadership would have none of those weaknesses in it. Sometimes they even rally such followers as they can get to enter into a civil war against the very group of Christians from whom they have just walked away.

Some years ago I opened my pulpit to an evangelist for a series of meetings. As is often the case, a few discontented members of the church got an audience with him and poured out their grievances. He instantly became their champion. The sermons became very pointed, and although he did not use my name, it was very obvious that he was attacking me. He seemed to have unlimited time to visit people in their homes, and he would gladly talk with anyone at length after the services. At the end of the week he announced that he was starting a church about ten miles from mine and took a group of people with him. He had united the people with his "come out from among them and join me" philosophy. Although we settled our differences long before his death, it is a classic example of uniting people by preying upon the weaknesses of others merely to build a personal kingdom.

There is a twist to this that is current today. Men with great personal ambition finance the building of their kingdoms by fleecing God's sheep. Violating the sanctity of the local church, they reach individuals by direct mail, radio, and television, making their pleas for donations "for the work of God." There is rarely an accounting made of how these funds are used, and too frequently the projects they "sell" never seem to come to fruition, but the appeals go on and on. They have a great variety of gimmicks with which to unite the people in giving, and their computers regularly spin out letters to the "faithful contributors," but the togetherness is false, the motivation is impure, and the end result is the financial well-being of the Absalom who is taking the money that belongs to the local church and putting it into his private kingdom. They may have brought a hundred thousand or more people together in a mailing list, but God's challenge to His leaders is to "feed My sheep," not fleece them.

Men need to get together, but too frequently their togetherness with one another is out of impure motives, for short-lived purposes and for personal gain. God has a much higher purpose for uniting His people.

Man's Getting Together With God

While getting together usually involves people with people, God desperately wants people to get together with Himself. The fellowship God enjoyed with Adam in Eden's garden was forfeited through sin, and God sent Jesus Christ to redeem men from sin in order to restore that intimate fellowship that was lost. Men need God. Men need fellowship with God. Mankind needs an intimate relationship with Almighty God, just to maintain a balance in day-to-day living. We were not made to be independent of God; we have a built-in dependency upon Him. Furthermore, we have a built-in awareness of this need for God, for all cultures in all geographic locations on this earth worship something or someone. Even the countries that proclaim atheism as their state religion have made the worship of the state their true religion. The human heart must worship; God made us worshiping creatures. If we do not worship God, we will worship people, ideologies, or things, but we will worship! We will strive to get together with something beyond ourselves and, hopefully, above ourselves. To the Christian this worship is a getting together with God in adoration, praise, humility, and submission, but we do not always get together with God with the purest motives.

Jacob—Genesis 28, 32

One example of this is Jacob at Bethel, and later at Peniel, where he had experiences with visiting angels. The first confrontation with angels was in his departure from his homeland as he fled from Esau's wrath at having lost not only the birthright but the family blessing as well. On Jacob's first night out, God appeared to him in a dream in which Jacob saw "a ladder set up on the earth, and the top of it reached to heaven: and behold the angels of God ascending and descending on it" (Genesis 28:12). He saw the Lord standing above the ladder, and the Lord spoke to him, promising him the land upon which he was lying plus blessings that extended into his posterity. When Jacob awakened with an awareness that indeed God was in that place, he made a pillar, poured oil on it, named the area Bethel, and vowed a vow that if God would prosper him, he would pay a tenth back to God (*see* Genesis 28:22). He reduced his meeting with God to a business proposition: "I'll give you a ten percent commission for all prosperity you give to me."

The second time Jacob had an intimate confrontation with God was on his return to his homeland. After making elaborate preparations to meet his angry brother Esau, he remained on the opposite side of the brook Jabbok ". . . and there wrestled a man with him until the breaking of the day" (Genesis 32:24). Hosea the prophet identifies this "man" as the angel of the Lord (*see* Hosea 12:4,5). When this representative of the Lord Jesus told Jacob to let Him go, Jacob answered, ". . . I will not let thee go, except thou bless me" (Genesis 32:26), and bless him He did. When it ended, Jacob was lame, renamed, and blessed, "and Jacob called the name of the place Peniel: for I have seen God face to face, and my life is preserved" (Genesis 32:30).

As requested, Jacob was blessed, but he was left alone. It is easier for us to understand how Jacob could be materialistically oriented in his first meeting with God, for he was young, without earthly goods, fleeing for his life, and terribly insecure. But in this second encounter with God he was returning to his homeland an exceedingly rich man. He had his wives, children, and servants with him, and he had re-

ceived Laban's blessing at Mizpeh. One would expect Jacob
to desire something more than material blessings from God,
especially when he had an all-night wrestling experience
with God.

In this refusal of Jacob to let the angel go until he received
a blessing, we watch an incidence of bargaining with God.
"You can have what you want from me if I can have what I
want from you" is the plea, and Jacob is not the last person
to make this appeal. It is all too common to hear similar
bargaining with God around the altars of prayer. In the
presence of God we try to execute a trade-off. How trivially
we trade the intimacy of God's presence for a momentary
blessing, whether emotional, physical, or financial! We prefer things of earthly value to things of heavenly worth. We
readily exchange the spiritual for the carnal and opt for the
temporal over the eternal. "What fools we mortals be."

God honored Jacob's faith and requests. In Haran God
prospered Jacob beyond his wildest imagination, even
though Laban changed Jacob's wages seven times. Following the Peniel experience the blessing of God continued in
Jacob's natural life. There was continued increase of his
herds and flocks; God protected him and gave him favor
with the inhabitants of the land in which Jacob settled; and
God made peace between Jacob and Esau. However, we do
not read of Jacob's having any further contacts with God.
He had had "faith for things" rather than "faith in God," so
he had to settle for living among his things instead of living
in the presence of God. Our generation that cherishes the
American dream of riches and ease seems more interested in
exercising faith for things than faith in God. Too frequently
a man's "spirituality" is judged by his possessions and
affluence. That one may bargain with God for material

blessings is proven in Jacob's life, but "things" are a very poor substitute for the presence of God.

It appears that many Christians seek a contract with God rather than a contact with Him. Surely God had something more lofty than a contract in mind when He revealed Himself to Jacob on two separate occasions, and it is equally certain that God has a higher purpose in intervening in our lives than to be brought into a ten percent contract to provide the things we need in this life. God wants fellowship. God desires communion with us. No contract is pleasing to God if it becomes a substitute for intimate contact with God. God would rather walk and talk with us than work for us. He would rather share our life than merely supply our life.

Jacob offered God a partnership instead of accepting a companionship. He let God share in the material gain of his life, but he did not share that life with God in a relationship. To make matters even worse, Jacob kept God as a silent partner. God had no voice in the "business"; He merely financed the operation and took His ten percent. To Jacob, God was far more his financier than his friend. God was his source of supply rather than the source of fellowship. In a limited sense Jacob was functioning together with God, but it was not the kind of togetherness that pleases God.

Any togetherness with God that finds us far more interested in "what's in it for me" than in "what's in it for God" falls far short of God's goals. That God yearns to get together with man is attested throughout all of the Scripture, but all too frequently man wants to get together with God only for material profit. Although Jacob saw God in the heavens in his youth, and in his middle years had personal and physical contact with Him, in neither incident could

Jacob express a desire for God's presence or for intimacy with God. Jacob wanted blessings—things! He would have fit very well in the American church of this generation. While it is indeed the "Father's good pleasure to give you the kingdom" (Luke 12:32), He is far more anxious to give us Himself. Seeking union with God for material gain is akin to a young woman's marrying an old man for his wealth. God desires better things of us than that!

Moses—Exodus 3

God got better things than that in the lives of other men. Moses, for example, never evidenced a desire for things once he met God at the burning bush. Perhaps it was because he had lived in the luxury of Egypt's palace, but there came a time when Moses put all of those things on the line to begin the emancipation of his brethren. The injustice of the slavery of the Hebrews and the realization that they were his people caused Moses to try to be their protector, provider, and liberator. He even slew an Egyptian on their behalf, but the Hebrews did not understand Moses' burning passion and deep concern for them, and they rejected him completely. Moses not only failed in his goal, but he had so committed himself as to anger Pharaoh, and he had to flee for his very life. For forty years this highly educated adopted son of Pharaoh's daughter lived in exile as a shepherd of his father-in-law's sheep.

Then God appeared to Moses in the burning bush and revived the old yearning to be a liberator by commissioning him to return to Egypt and do exactly what he had proposed to do forty years before. Only this time Moses was to function under the direct orders of God. Now Moses discovered that God's strength was inexorably coupled with this divine call. It would not be a mere Moses delivering Israel; it would be God and Moses. A partnership in service was formed at this burning bush. God needed a man, and this man desperately needed God. Both of them had similar visions, but each needed the other to fulfill that vision.

This time, in partnership with God, Moses succeeded gloriously. With the sign of the rod's becoming a serpent and then a rod again, and a hand that became leprous when placed in his bosom and was made whole again by repeating that act, Moses dared to return to Egypt to confront Pharaoh. But Pharaoh wasn't very impressed. He considered the signs Moses showed him to be little more than sleight of hand, and the court magicians duplicated them. Instead of fleeing as before, Moses returned to God's presence for further instructions, and God told him to threaten Pharaoh with a plague. When the threat didn't work, Moses stretched forth the rod that Pharaoh had refused to see as a divine implement, and the promised plague appeared.

Although Pharaoh gave in to the pressure of earlier plagues, he always changed his mind, because, the Scriptures affirm, God hardened his heart (*see* Exodus 4:21; 7:3; 14:4). Having been forewarned of God that this would happen, Moses was forearmed and merely sent plague after plague upon Egypt. Over and over this was repeated until Pharaoh finally relented and released the slaves. Paramount among the many things God accomplished in these delays was repeated communication and fellowship with Moses. This chosen vessel of God was learning complete dependence upon God and was learning to be content in getting his orders on a day-to-day basis. Every refusal of Pharaoh left Moses without further alternative. He had done everything God had told him to, and it didn't appear to work, so he had to go back to God, for unlike Jacob, who had entered into a contract with God, Moses functioned out of a contact with God. He received verbal orders and obeyed them.

God and Moses worked this partnership during the continuation of the life of Moses. Whatever the need, Moses would take it to God, and from this communication with God came judgments for the people, guidance for their journey, and provision for their daily sustenance. While the people always held Moses responsible, God consistently reassured Moses that they were actually rebelling against God, their unseen Leader. For the forty years that Moses led the people in the wilderness, God initiated the action, and Moses implemented it. They were an unbeatable team.

It is likely that Moses' initial failure became a key to his subsequent success, for he learned that without God he could do nothing. Jesus taught us the same principle when He said, ". . . apart from me you can do nothing" (John 15:5 RSV). It seems, from personal observation, that a very high percentage of those who enter the service of God function apart from Him. They both initiate the action and implement it. They are zealous, often highly trained and efficient, and they are self-motivated, but they are working FOR God rather than WITH God. They have a compassion for the need and a consecration to the task, but they have not yet developed a relationship with God. They have never learned that "we are labourers together with God" (1 Corinthians 3:9). They are responding to a precept rather than to a person.

Even though they may attain a measure of success, they miss God's highest purpose—getting together with Him! The work of the Lord on earth is more an opportunity for man and God to get together in activity than it is a prime necessity. If God could create this world with His Word, He certainly could perform His work with His Word, but He chooses to do it through His men and women in order that He can have fellowship, communion, conversation, and consultation with them. It creates a need for togetherness. God let Moses fail in his self-energized effort in order to force dependence upon God, and this same merciful God has allowed many workers to fail miserably for the very same purpose. God would like all of our labors to be together with Him, but even more than this, He would like all of our lives to be entwined with His life.

Abraham—Genesis 12

Several generations before Moses, God had a man who lived in intimate fellowship with Him. Abraham dwelt among the idolators of Ur of Chaldea when he heard the voice of God calling him out of that land to walk with God in an undesignated place. In blind obedience, Abraham left his home and country and set out to walk with God. Although God made repeated promises of a land that would be given to Abraham's progeny, Abraham himself was seemingly unaware of receiving it, for he lived nomadically in tents, always looking forward to the fulfillment of God's promises in his life. It did not seem that he was motivated by prosperity, although God made him an exceedingly rich man, nor did Abraham enter into any great divine service. Abraham simply walked with God. Repeatedly we read of his building an altar to God. Angels were dispatched to talk with him, and on Mount Moriah God Himself talked with him. Abraham was not called to do great things for God; he was called to live a life of obedience to God. Fellowship with God was his main forte, and God loved it. "... Abra-

ham believed God, and it was imputed unto him for righteousness: and he was called the Friend of God" (James
2:23). Abraham did not need to be a doer; he was a believer,
and his simple obedience to God brought him into such a
warm relationship with God that he became a friend of
God.

Some of what God had enjoyed with Adam in the garden
was to be found in His relationship with Abraham. They
simply enjoyed each other. Abraham wasn't using God, and
God wasn't particularly using Abraham. They primarily
walked together throughout Abraham's long life as friend
with friend. Abraham learned the highest reward of getting
together with God: friendship!

God will give unto us if we insist on a contract, and He
will work with us if we insist on a partnership, but God
would rather get together with man on the simple terms of a
friendship. God prefers worshipers to workers and intimacy
to activity. Some people have learned to like what God
likes, and they get together with Him for His highest purpose. These have a special place in God's heart.

Man does get together both with other men and with
God, but far too often his purpose for getting together is far
beneath God's double-decker purpose for uniting us. God
has both a utilitarian purpose and an ultimate purpose for
getting us together and since God is sovereign, His purposes
will prevail.

2

God's *Utilitarian* Purpose for Getting Us Together

As laudable as man's purposes for getting together may be, they are miniscule and selfish when compared to the divine purposes for uniting man with man, man with God, and heaven with earth. The goal of God's redemptive program in Christ Jesus is not merely that men may escape hell, but that the redeemed may come into such an intimate relationship with God that they may begin to know God. Out of such personal acquaintance can come an unfolding of the wisdom of God. That is the declaration Paul makes here in Ephesians 1:9 in writing, "Having made known unto us the mystery of his will, according to his good pleasure which he hath purposed in himself." God's higher goal of redemption is to restore man to a place where he is able to understand the mystery of the divine will—to know, not merely believe.

The Divine Purpose Explained

This word *mystery* seems to be one of Paul's favorite words, for he uses it at least twenty times in his New Testament writings. Each time, he uses the Greek word *musterion,* which comes from the root word *mustes,* referring to the secret societies of the Greeks. Hence, *musterion* is that which is known to the *mustes.* As with the teachings of America's secret orders, such as the Masonic Lodge, where one must be initiated to higher and higher degrees in order to learn higher levels of the "secrets" of the lodge, Paul is suggesting that knowing the mysteries of God depends upon commitment to God, and that our level of knowing will be more dependent upon our consecration than upon our concentration.

The New Testament usage of the word *mystery* does not denote the mysterious (as seems to be the common usage of the English word in our society today) but signifies, as we've already seen, that which can be known only by divine revelation, and this comes only to the initiated. Certainly Paul is not referring to closed communion groups such as we have in our generation who will teach only those who are "submitted" or "committed" to certain leaders. Paul merely suggests that the work of the cross has initiated us into God. The death of our sinful self and the impartation of divine life have taken us out of the common life and have put us in the very uncommon; it is from the natural into the spiritual. This work of grace, this action of the cross, opens us to be the recipients of the mysteries of God.

Surely there is no mystery about that of which we have no knowledge at all. The jet plane, for instance, was no mystery to Paul, for there wasn't sufficient scientific development in his day to even provoke such imaginativeness. Similarly, then, there can be no spiritual mystery where there is no knowledge at all. Unless God begins to unlock the secret by sharing at least a glimpse into the unknown, we will have no basis for searching into new dimensions of spiritual truth.

It is equally true that there cannot be any mystery about anything of which we have full knowledge. Having purchased a home computer, I can honestly confess that there are still many mysteries about its workings that puzzle me; but we have men in our congregation who are computer programmers, to whom the computer is but a common tool whose mysteries were long ago revealed to them. I am quite certain that some of my questions seem very childish and basic to them, but that is because what is no longer a mystery to them is still very much of an unknown quotient to me much of the time. What I have learned so far only causes me to know how much more there is to learn. Even so, God's Word has that marvelous capacity to unfold part of the truth—just enough to make us aware that there is much more to be learned.

God's wisdom will always be a mystery to man, if for no other reason than the fact that it flows from an infinite mind that man's finite mind can only partly grasp. Just as a child's entrance into school opens a vast realm of the unknown that requires years of teaching before he can actually know it, so God first has to expose us and then teach us progressively. The prophet Isaiah seemed to grasp this principle when he wrote, "Whom shall he teach knowledge? and whom shall he make to understand doctrine? them that are weaned from the milk, and drawn from the breasts. For precept must be upon precept, precept upon precept; line upon line, line upon line; here a little, and there a little" (Isaiah 28:9,10).

God's plan for the Church is a mystery both because it is revealed in part and because it is not fully revealed. In *Clarke's Commentary,* Dr. Adam Clarke writes, "That the Gentiles should ever be received into the Church of God, and have all the privileges of the Jews, without being obliged to submit to circumcision, and perform the rites and ceremonies of the Jewish law was a *mystery—a hidden thing* which had never been published before; and *now* revealed

only to the apostles. It was *God's will* that it should be so, but
He kept that will *hidden* to the present time." I find it easy to
believe that there is very likely a time when the world in
general, and men in particular, are really not ready for
God's mysteries. Rather than expound them, God uses them
to stimulate a sober and devout inquisitiveness in minds that
have been blunted by sin. As in the case of Martin Luther,
these unexplained mysteries prod the mind to fresh research
and stir the soul to renewed vigor in seeking God. Not only
will an awareness of a mystery stimulate inquisitiveness, but
it will also humble the individual reasonings. God loves to
prove to men that they cannot unlock spiritual mysteries by
scientific research or philosophical reasoning. The world of
mankind must undergo much preparation before a divine
mystery can be unraveled.

But Paul was not speaking of divine mysteries in general
so much as he was specifically speaking of the great mystery
of the Church. As Paul saw it, the true mystery of the
Church is not merely that the Gentiles would be included in
it, for the Old Testament prophetic Scriptures seem to expound this truth quite consistently. But it was not known
until after the day of Pentecost that the theocracy itself was
going to be dismantled and abolished, and that a new dispensation was to be established under which the old distinc-
tion of Jew and Gentile was to be removed. It was not the
purpose of God to add the Gentile to the Jew; His higher
purpose was to break down the walls and barriers that separated them and to make of both one new man (*see* Ephesians 2:14,15). It is "that one new man" that is the true mystery of the New Testament.

Christ is God's mystery, and yet this has been missed by
many Christians in spite of thousands of books that have

been written about Jesus. For the most part, today's Christians are locked in the Gospels when they think about Jesus, failing to see beyond the cradle and the cross. They do not see Him as a revelation of the Father, nor as the vehicle whereby you, I, we, and they can lose individual identities and become partakers of His life and participants in His Body here on earth.

That the Church itself is not the full mystery of the Gospel is made evident in chapter 3 of Ephesians, where Paul declares that the Church is to be the channel through which God will reveal the mystery. He writes, "And to make all men see what is the fellowship of the mystery, which from the beginning of the world hath been hid in God, who created all things by Jesus Christ; to the intent that now unto the principalities and powers in heavenly places might be known *by the church* the manifold wisdom of God" (Ephesians 3:9,10, italics added).

God does not seem to have chosen any vehicle for the revelation of His mystery other than the Church. Demonstrably God's Word does not reveal this mystery to the world, for that Word itself is a mystery to the unbeliever. God's Word is the channel God uses for the preparing of His Church, but it is that Church that is the vehicle for the revelation of the mystery of God. If Christ is not revealed in our life as an individual, and in our lives collectively as we learn to get together as a true body of believers in Christ Jesus, then the mystery will never be known. Therefore, we who often divide ourselves with doctrines must learn to unite ourselves in Christ Jesus, for Jesus Christ, who is God's mystery, is also the key to the solution of the mystery—the spiritual, intellectual, and moral mystery of the world.

Jesus is not entirely new; He is the fresh factor introduced

into the equation. In most philosophies and religions God
and man have always been. Whether God is viewed as a
Supreme Being or merely as a "first cause" or a "pervading
principle," all thought patterns must eventually go back to a
beginning, and that beginning is God. Furthermore, there
has always been man, whether seen as a developing proto-
plasm or as a specific creation. Now there is a new God and
a new Man—"the man Christ Jesus" (1 Timothy 2:5).

God with us—"Emmanuel"—had become accepted.
Throughout the Old Testament men learned the reality of
the presence of God in their daily lives. The cloud, manna,
and water for Israel in the wilderness established this pattern. God *in* man is what was new, while man in God was an
undiscovered mystery until Paul's day. One hundred sixty-
four times the New Testament speaks of our being "in
Christ." I know of no one other truth in the New Testament
that is spoken of more frequently than this, for this is the
mystery of the Gospel—individuals of greatly different heri-
tages and cultures placed in Christ to become the visible
"Body of Christ" here on the earth. Not only did God become man, but through this incarnation, provision has been
made for man to come into God. What a glorious mystery!
Only God could effect it, and only we can reveal it.

Jesus Christ is, indeed, God's last word to this world.
Whether understanding comes through seeing Jesus in the
Gospels, or a revelation of Christ in the Epistles, or merely
through the ministry of the Church, its true source is Jesus
Christ. Whether sunlight, candlelight, or electricity, the
source of light is the sun, and whether revelation comes
from above directly or through involvement with the earthly
Body of Christ in the Church, it is a revelation from God.

Hence Jesus the mystery becomes Christ the solution to

that mystery. I wonder if we are not getting close to a time when the politicians, theoreticians, and economists are going to turn to the Church and say, "We have tried everything that we know, but nothing works. Do you have any suggestions? Is there an answer in your God?" I hope by that time the Church will not merely recite her doctrinal creeds but will be so united spiritually that she can dare to declare Christ to be the answer to every problem in life because He has so completely met every need in human experience.

Jesus is the light, the illumination, and the revelation of the mystery of God that is so desperately needed in our world today. Without Him men still walk in darkness. Without Him our minds are clouded in a fog of ignorance, but His presence dispels the darkness and pierces the clouds in men's minds to bring revelation back into the experiences of men.

God intends to get all things back under the authority of the Lord Jesus Christ both as He is seated at the right hand of God the Father and as He is living here on this earth in His Church, which is declared to be His Body (*see* 1 Corinthians 12:27).

Pleasured Purposes

While the God-man may have been a mystery to men throughout the ages of time, it delights the heart of God to pull the wraps off this unknown quotient and to reveal Jesus to "whosoever." Paul said, "Having made known unto us the mystery of his will, according to his *good pleasure* which he hath purposed in himself" (Ephesians 1:9, italics added). It is relaxing for us to know that the whole scheme of redemption and revelation gives God pleasure, for this helps us to believe in its perpetuity. Restoring fallen creation is not a painful process but a pleasured purpose of God's own choosing. "He has made known to us his hidden purpose— such was his will and pleasure determined beforehand in Christ . . ." the New English Bible translates this verse. Furthermore, the planning and the revelation of this mystery were not influenced by any external consideration whatsoever. The whole reason for it sprang from within God Himself. It is "according to his good pleasure *which he hath purposed in himself"* (italics added). God did it without foreign aid or human intercession.

This purpose that gives such pleasure to God is to form a united kingdom consisting of the unfallen and the restored—a uniting of the things in heaven and the things on the earth in Christ Jesus. God wants to restore in Christ a lost unity! He purposes to bring together disunited elements that were segmented as a result of the introduction of sin.

God has had a scheme, a plan, a purpose from before the foundation of the world and running through all the ages. He is going to bring back to Himself everything that pulled away from Him. While not all will come back into loving harmony, all will come back into submissive obedience. The true purpose of the life history of man, and indeed of all history, was made plain in Jesus Christ: *He* was the crown, the climax, the supreme achievement in heaven above and earth beneath, and nothing is going to keep that revelation from being made manifest, for God gets great pleasure in revealing it.

Throughout the history of the world God has found great pleasure in executing His plan. In passage after passage Paul speaks of God patiently and determinedly working through all the ages to accomplish His great and loving purpose. This purpose, as translated by Dr. Richard Francis Weymouth, is ". . . of restoring the whole creation to find its one head in Christ" (Ephesians 1:10).

There is a current Christian philosophy that says that in the end time God is going to fulfill all of His purposes. This view teaches that in the last days there will be great persecution, great revival, great ingathering, great purification, and so forth. While all of this will likely occur in the end times, it seems inconsistent with God's revelation to assume that it will occur *only* in the end of time. God began His plan of restoration in the garden of Eden, and every age, every period of time, every sector of human history, and every person whose feet have touched the ground have been part of God's processes. God has been working His purposes from beginning to end. Frequently those who play a part in God's purposes don't have a clue that they are involved in a divine program, for God has a marvelous ability to cause unbelievers to serve His purposes gloriously. They may not serve Him in love, but they will serve His purposes nonetheless, whether consciously or unconsciously.

Paul did not view the past generations as wasted, unused years of failure. He saw them as years in which God was pursuing His unchanging purpose, not only of rescuing a few exceptional individuals from the wreckage produced by the fall, but of restoring the whole creation, and he saw it operating throughout the whole period of man's history. Little by little, ". . . line upon line . . ." God was revealing His plan. We take great pride in our generation because our knowledge is so great. But we frequently fail to realize the accumulation of the stored-up knowledge of the centuries that have preceded us. We are not the first people to have come into knowledge, but we were able to begin our discoveries at the point where past seekers left off. This is true both naturally and spiritually.

Our generation is blessed with a written record of the revelations God has made of Himself and His plan throughout preceding generations of mankind. God's revelation is built progressively, and we are the richer because of past revealings. Certainly, then, God has not waited until the end of time to begin His program of redemption and revelation. To the church at Rome Paul wrote, "The creature itself also shall be delivered from the bondage of corruption into the glorious liberty of the children of God" (Romans 8:21). Nothing has been wasted, for even the wreckage produced by the fall will find complete restoration into the purposes of God. Hence Jesus Christ furnishes the key to the past as well as to the future.

Dispensational Determination

Paul introduces yet another concept into his argument that Jesus Christ is God's mysterious answer to getting all things back together again. Having declared that God had purposed to do this, he adds, "That in the dispensation of the fulness of times . . ." (Ephesians 1:10). The Greek word he uses, which we have translated as "dispensation," is *oikonomia,* which is a combination of two other Greek words: *oikos,* "a house," and *nomos,* "a law." Basically, then, the word refers to the management of household affairs. It is a matter of the administration of the property of others. It is stewardship. In his *Expository Dictionary of New Testament Words,* W. E. Vine tells us, "A dispensation is not a period or epoch (a common, but erroneous, use of the word), but a mode of dealing, an arrangement or administration of affairs." So Paul is not speaking of an epoch during which God has been gathering things together in Christ, but he is referring to the fundamental administration of God's affairs in effecting this togetherness.

Adam Clarke says that the word *oikonomia* ". . . is the same as our word *economy.*" Hence it is "in God's economy of the fullness of times. . . ." Beck translates this tenth verse, ". . . to manage everything in heaven and on earth in such a way that when the right time would come it would all be organized under Christ as its Head." God's management program covers from eternity to eternity (not merely from the beginning of time to the end of time). God is not locked into our time-space dimension. God had this program drawn up long before time began.

Just as there is in creation a unity of plan with certain ideas and regulative numbers forming its essence, so there is in God's administration a specific succession of times and seasons working out the purposes of His will. More and more, science is unlocking these "laws" of nature—mathematical exactness that God used in the specific creation. Similarly, there are "laws" of the same exactness working to bring God's purpose of uniting everything together in Christ Jesus into actuality. God so manages His household that nothing is allowed to get out of His control. He regulates the affairs and actions of men so that they contribute to God's program, and He vetoes anything that works contrary to His will. As Dr. Luke put it, "[God] hath made of one blood all nations of men for to dwell on all the face of the earth, and hath determined the times before appointed, and the bounds of their habitation" (Acts 17:26).

Any political ruler or governmental agency that insists on moving in a direction opposed to the purposes of God is quickly eradicated. God still controls the breath man breathes, and it is no problem for Him to withdraw life from the one who will not follow the divine plan. This does not take anything away from the free will of man, but that free will cannot take anything away from the sovereignty of God, either. It is God who has determined the bounds, the times, and the seasons. God has always made good use of His seasons. Paul reminds us, "But when the fulness of the time was come, God sent forth his Son . . ." (Galatians 4:4). Similarly, it was "due time" when Christ died for the ungodly, for His actual death at Calvary coincided with the time set for the slaying of the Paschal lamb. Furthermore, it will be in "the time appointed" that Christ will return in clouds of great glory to receive His waiting Church unto Himself. God has preprogrammed His timing, and He controls the affairs of men to bring about His own divine purposes.

God is a good manager or administrator. He works according to a plan; He has the power to implement that plan, and He has the times and seasons in His control for the revelation of that plan. Whatever He sets out to do, He accomplishes. Nothing can hinder Him; none can prevent His purposes. Paul wrote, "Being confident of this very thing, that he which hath begun a good work in you *will perform it* until the day of Jesus Christ" (Philippians 1:6, italics added).

The Divine Purpose Extended

When Paul wrote, "That . . . he might gather together in one all things in Christ . . ." (Ephesians 1:10), he certainly alluded to the experiential and the practical as well as to the prophetic. Although there is an *ultimate* purpose (to be examined in the next chapter), there is also a very *utilitarian* purpose in God's bringing things together again. Beyond the philosophical lies the practical, and most of us need to benefit from God's provision in a personal manner before we are interested or qualified to grasp its philosophical implications.

Individuals Getting Their Lives Together

While God's ultimate purpose is to unite in Christ everything in heaven and on earth, God begins on the smaller utilitarian plane of getting men together with Christ singly and then unitedly. Large programs are merely many small programs amalgamated under a master plan, and while we may not comprehend the whole, we can participate in the partial.

Perhaps the beginning point in the revealing of God's mystery is in the divine provision for people to get their lives together. There is a tremendous cry in our generation from people asking, "Who am I? What is the purpose of life? Why am I here?" We have watched a large segment of our generation withdraw from reality, trying to philosophically determine who they were. Others merely rejected life as they had been shown it, opting for drugs, rock music, sexual promiscuity, and drink. Our generation seems to have a craving, and I believe it to be a God-imparted craving, for people to try to get their lives together and to discover the meaning of life. Whether this is in spite of, or because of, the tremendous breakdown in the home structure in America and the repeated failures of marriages and personal attainment socially, economically, and spiritually doesn't matter so much as the fact that people are now trying to "get their act together." But history shows that it will not come through self-discovery or knowledge of psychiatry or psychology. There is only one way God has provided for any of us to "get our act together" and to discover who we are, and that is to get in Christ, for until we have been united with Christ Jesus we will never really know who we are or why we are here on earth.

If the funds are available, an individual may, through the services of a skilled psychiatrist, find out who he *was*, but by the time the therapy is completed the person may very well have changed. It is only retrospectively that any of us have any understanding of ourselves, but when we get into Christ Jesus we not only discover what we were, but by the work of His cross we come to know what we are, and by the Spirit we come to know what we are becoming. Religion is not, as Lenin charged, the opiate of the people; it is the illumination of the people. Until the Spirit comes to take residence in our lives, we believers have no understanding of who we are. It is the Spirit who searches the deep things of the heart and life, and He lets us know what is the mind of God. I cannot know the true "me" without being in Christ!

As a pastor I have found that if I can get people to touch God, rather than touch me, there comes an unveiling of the real life that God has put within them, and an understanding that we are made in His likeness, in His image, are recipients of His grace, are filled with His goodness, and are moving into His glory. It takes this knowledge and His grace to help us get our lives together.

Far too often our own personal *self* is a divided kingdom. There frequently is distraction and division where there ought to be peace and harmony. Each of us is a very complex individual with conscience, will, imagination, desire, and passions that often pull in distinctly different directions and create great upheaval within us. To counter this inner competition, all of a person's spirit, all of his soul, and all of his body must be gathered together as one unit in Christ Jesus. Perhaps one of the underlying causes for so much divorce in America is the prevailing concept that marriage makes up the whole; but the Bible teaches that it is Christ Jesus who makes us a complete individual. While marriage is a completing factor in life, it is not totally completing, for marriage does not fulfill the spirit of an individual—only God can do that—and marriage is confined to the body-soul needs of individuals.

If you were to walk into a band room before the bandmaster arrived, you would very likely walk into sheer bedlam. Each musician is tuning his instrument, or merely playing a portion of a piece that is especially familiar to him. Each member is doing his own thing, thereby producing discord and confusion. But when that bandmaster mounts the podium and taps his baton for attention, the individual wills of the musicians are surrendered to the will of the conductor, and this one will controls all so that disunity becomes harmony and distraction gives way to enjoyment as the band plays a familiar Sousa march.

Similarly, when the Lord Jesus Christ comes into a man's being, the discords and pains, the individual rioting and confusion give way to the controlling divine will, bringing fellowship and harmony. But even more than this, Christ not only controls but pervades the instrumentalists! Unlike the bandmaster who has nothing more than external authority going for him, Christ's Spirit enters man's conscience, will, emotions, affections, senses, and even the flesh and makes them Christlike so that the man no longer functions merely because he is surrendering to the will of God; he does it because Jesus is living in his conscience, He is liv-

ing in his will, He is living in his mind, He is living in man's
spirit and is even abiding in man's flesh. Christ cannot dwell
in human bodies without the very bodies themselves being
sanctified. Paul asks, "Know ye not that your body is the
temple of the Holy Ghost? . . ." (1 Corinthians 6:19). When
Christ comes into the life, distraction gives place to unity,
discord becomes harmony, and the once-alien powers kneel
together around a common head, Jesus Christ; we find ourselves united as individuals because all our faculties are
brought to peace in God.

This is what happens when in terror, we pray; when in
confusion, we seek God. We simply allow God to bring
every function of our being back into unity in Him, and we
come to peace with ourselves; this makes it possible to be at
peace with our fellow man, which, in turn, makes peace with
God possible and plausible.

Getting the Home Together

If the mystery of God's will is to get everything together
in Christ, then in the utilitarian outworking of this we must
begin to get our homes together, for the home is the smallest
unit of the church. While Jesus said, "For where two or
three are gathered together in my name, there am I in the
midst of them" (Matthew 18:20), I like to think of it as
"where *he* and *she* are gathered together," for that was the
way it was in the garden of Eden in the beginning. A Christian husband and wife become both the smallest unit of a
church and the building block that comprises God's great
Church here on earth. As every pastor can attest, the spiritual strength of a local church cannot rise above the
strength of the homes that make up that local congregation,

for the strength of the whole is determined by the strengths of its parts.

Among the shocks awaiting the newly married couple's return from the honeymoon is the discovery that the home is filled with divisive forces. While it may be true that love is blind, it is equally true that marriage is an eye-opener, for when the committed parties set themselves to the task of blending their lives together to form a Christian home, they soon learn that there are vast differences between them. These diversities become even more apparent as children increase the membership of the home. Even in those who have the same genes, there will be great dissimilarities in attitudes, aptitudes, and abilities.

It is foolish to ignore the many differences within the home. There are, obviously, physical differences. Some members of the home may be physically strong while others may be physically weak, and this can be a very divisive force, especially if the strong expects the weak to keep up the same pace, or if the weak become resentful at the stamina of the strong. Some individuals by nature have nerves like steel, and others have tensed nerves like tender violin strings—they're always vibrating—and this contrast can become divisive. Equally, there are vast differences in temperament, for it is rare that two individuals of the same temperament get together in marriage, thanks to the working of the law that "opposites attract." Somehow you rarely see two "spoons" nestled together in marriage; it is usually a "knife" and a "fork."

There will often be a great divergence of aptitudes in the home. One member may be very mechanical, while a second member is artistic. The artistic person may not even be able to hang the picture he has painted, while the mechanically inclined member of the home can frame the picture he is unable to appreciate. Still another may be happily domestic, while a fourth has a strong musical aptitude, and this can create tensions. The musician may resent having to use the vacuum, while the domestically oriented person cannot understand the ineptness of the musician in the kitchen. Furthermore, each individual member of the family has a distinct will that is active. They do not mature into having a will; they are born with it!

All of these contrarieties and contrasts must be brought together, or there is not going to be peace in the home. One way we hear about to bring this all together is to teach, practice, and enforce the headship of the man—"headship" being interpreted as "lordship" or "dictatorship"—but this extreme teaching is very artificial. It doesn't bring things together in the home; it merely keeps things from being expressed. It is far more profitable, and scriptural, for all these potentially divisive forces in the home to be gathered together in one "in Christ." The physical factors, the temperaments, the aptitudes, and the wills all need to be surrendered to Christ; they need to be Christ-ruled and Christ-pervaded. They need to be Christianized; they need to be sanctified, and when they are, the mechanical person and the artistic person have a common denominator in Christ. The iron will and the violin string can function together "in Christ." This will not erase the individualities; actually they will be illumined and glorified. God does not put a family in a Christian melting pot and pour us all into the same mold; God created individuality and He goes to great lengths to preserve it. But the coming of Christ into the home and the indwelling of the Spirit of Christ in each individual member converts the home into a miniature heaven. Without it, it is likely that the diverse individuals will cause that home to degenerate into a living hell. God's will is the former, not the latter, and to effect it He has made it possible for the home to get together "in Christ."

Getting the Church Together

It would be dangerously incomplete to consider the utilitarian purpose for togetherness if we did not look, at least briefly, at God's provision to get the Church on earth together, at least to the point where it is not divided because of its differences. This book of Ephesians espouses the gathering of the Church into one great Body, and Paul addresses the major division of his day: the division between the Jews and the Gentiles in the Church. In chapter 2 Paul speaks of the great contrast between the Circumcision and the Uncircumcision (verse 11) and refers to the Gentiles as "having no hope, and without God in the world" (verse 12), and then declares, "But now in Christ Jesus ye who sometimes were far off are made nigh by the blood of Christ. For he is our peace, who hath made both one, and hath broken down the middle wall of partition between us; having abolished in his flesh the enmity, . . . for to make in himself of twain one new man; so making peace" (verses 13–15). While we often make application of this passage in many directions, Paul was specifically addressing the Jew-Gentile issue, and he declared that God was making them both one. The wall that had separated them was "broken down." It was not so much that they were merging, but that each was becoming "one new man."

What Paul was saying was that there cannot be a Jewish and a Gentile Church; there is only Christ's Church. Similarly, then, there cannot be the American Church and the African Church, if, indeed, we have become members of Christ's Church. We have been united in Christ. We have been brought into "one new man." No denomination is that "new man," nor can any individual become that "new man." *Christ* is God's "new man." The true Church itself is not that "new man"; it is only the Body of that man—and Christ Himself is its Head.

If, then, all Christians have been placed "in Christ" and have become members of His Body here on earth, the divisions among us must give way to unity. Doctrinal differences must be set aside, for although we may not come into a unity of concept for quite a while, we have come into a unity of function in our separate relationships in Christ Jesus. While there will remain ecclesiastical diversities, they dare not be allowed to be divisional. Styles of worship, forms of government, and sectarian views on eschatology dare not be the basis for the breaking of fellowship. There are not many Churches; there is one! The many and varied groups and individuals in the Church mystical are being united into "one new man."

Christ gave Himself for the Church—it is His Church—and He will ever be its center and gravitational core, and we must learn to allow ourselves to be pulled into the unity of being "one man" in Christ Jesus. The unity of the Church will become a revelation of the glory of the Father in Jesus Christ. In His high priestly prayer Jesus said, "That they all may be one; as thou, Father, art in me, and I in thee, that they also may be one in us: that the world may believe that thou hast sent me. And the glory which thou gavest me I have given them; that they may be one, even as we are one: I in them, and thou in me, that they may be made perfect in one; and that the world may know that thou hast sent me, and hast loved them, as thou hast loved me" (John 17:21–23).

When we do get together—when the entire Church is united as the Family of God—the world will have to recognize that God did indeed send Jesus, for they will begin to see the glory of the Father in the Body of Jesus here on the earth. It will not be by our doctrine or our books, but by our holding together as a united core of believers around the Lord Jesus Christ as that manifest Body of the Lord on this earth that the glory of God is going to be seen again.

God's goal is that the entire Church be united so it can function as the Body of Christ. If we refuse a unity of choice, we may be brought into a unity of necessity. God can make us get together out of a common need one for another, for He is as great a need maker as He is a need meeter, so if we will join together only out of need, He so controls the politics, economics, and physical factors of this earth that He can easily set up a situation where the Church will get together for survival.

Getting All Things Together "in Christ"

God yearns for a restored fellowship. While during the past ten years there has been a heavy conference emphasis on "getting together," the focus of that emphasis has been on getting you and me together, but the scriptural emphasis is that of you and me getting together with God. When Christians unite in fellowshipping Christ, they will also enjoy personal fellowship one with another; hence God yearns for restored fellowship with His Church here on earth. Many local congregations have learned to fellowship one with another, but few churches seem to know how to enter into a true fellowship with the Lord. We can sing songs about Him, but true communication with Him is unfortunately rare. God hungers for a better relationship between the Head in heaven and the Body here on earth.

Furthermore, Christ longs to spiritually complete us. Many of our problems as individuals exist because we are so incomplete. We've sought completion in friendship, in activity, in education, and in marriage, but it can be found only in the Lord Jesus Christ. "Ye are complete in Him . . ." (Colossians 2:10) the Scripture declares, and God wants to complete the individual with salvation and the indwelling Spirit. God also wants to complete the home with His sanctity and life. Much has been written about what is being forfeited in the American home by the loss of family ties through much moving and through divorce, but we need a fresh awakening to what is lost when the home really doesn't have fellowship with Christ. While grandparents can contribute some things, God can contribute all things. What may be lacking in human relationship may gloriously be made up for us in divine relationship. God would love to complete the home, make it a whole unit, and set it up as a demonstration to the world of what a real home can be.

God also purposes to complete the Church with His gifts and gifted men. Organization and mobilization can never substitute for the divine provisions God has made for His Church. Since the Church is His Body on earth, it must function in His life. A church without the life and giftings of the Spirit of God is as incomplete as a motor without fuel or a robot without a battery. All of our outward forms and ministries are dependent upon an inward life, and Christ is that life by His Spirit.

In getting all things together "in Christ," God not only

seeks to restore fellowship and spiritually complete us; He earnestly desires to reveal Himself to us. Individually He wants to reveal Himself to us as a Bridegroom lover. To the home He wants to reveal Himself as a true Father, and in the Church He wants to be revealed as the Head of the Church, the Life of the Church, and the object of the spiritual responses of the Church. God wants us to know Him, not merely know about Him.

God's method of accomplishing all of this is to "gather together in one all things in Christ. . . ." When all are *in* Him then all are *of* Him, *for* Him, and *by* Him. Either we start *in* Him, or nothing is *of, for,* or *by* Him. When we are *in* Him we all learn of the same Teacher, live by the same life, are energized by the same Spirit, and are motivated by the same will. This becomes such a uniting force and harmonizing agent as to make any church productive and any family peaceful.

Our vision of the divine is always proportional to our togetherness with Christ. The greater the exercise of our self-will, the smaller will be our true involvement with things divine; but the more the life is submerged in God, the greater will be the harmony and victory for the individual, and the wider will be the channel for a revelation of God and His ultimate purposes for the individual, the home, the Church, and the world.

3

God's *Ultimate* Purpose for Getting Us Together

Because we are finite beings desperately trying to understand something of the infinite, we tend to embrace the usefulness of truth without probing the depths of that truth. We seek to grasp what is good for our goals without exploring God's goals. We stop at the introduction of the good without exploring that which is best. How easily this could be true of our attempt to understand why God is trying to get us together. We rejoice at the accrued blessings of individuals getting their lives together, of couples putting their homes together, of pastors getting the church together, and of believers benefiting by getting all things together "in Christ." But as high as this is, it is not God's highest. It has a utilitarian purpose, but it is not God's *ultimate* purpose.

In his letter to the church at Ephesus, Paul wrote, "That in the dispensation of the fulness of times he might gather together in one all things in Christ, both which are in heaven, and which are on earth; even in him" (Ephesians 1:10), or, as J. B. Phillips translates it, "For God has allowed us to know the secret of His Plan, and it is this: He purposes in His sovereign will that all human history shall be consummated in Christ, that everything that exists in Heaven or earth shall find its perfection and fulfilment in Him" (Ephesians 1:9,10 PHILLIPS).

The Presumptions in This Verse

Paul's statement that Christ is going to "gather together in one all things in Christ, both which are in heaven, and which are on earth" implies at least three things. It certainly presumes that all things were once united together in one, assuming that angels and men were united to God by the ties of creation, for all were made by His Word and were under the same laws of nature. There was peace and friendship between them, and this harmonious relationship embraced both God and each other. Paul believed that God created everything in perfect unity.

A second presumption in this verse is that it assumes a disunion and a scattering of things in the heavens and things on the earth, for we never have to gather that which has not been scattered. If once things were in the basket and now we must gather up and replace those things in the basket, something must have upset that basket. This verse surmises that something separated men from God and from good angels, and even suggests that there was a separation of angel from angel. It further acknowledges that there has been a separation of men from men, for the theme of Ephesians is the separation of the Jews and Gentiles from one another. It believes that every man has turned to his own way, thereby precipitating separation one from another. Paul hardly needed to be a theologian to believe in the disunion and scattering of men from angels, God, and one another. Observation of life around him would teach him this.

A third presumption in this verse is the suggestion that

there will be a gathering of them together again, because it clearly states that "he might gather together in one all things in Christ. . . ." It deduces that man and God can be rejoined in companionship, that man and angels can be reunited in fellowship, and that man and man can be restored to comradeship. While it is the declared purpose of Satan to divide, it is the dedicated work of the Spirit to unite. There is probably no greater need for studying unity than when we are experiencing division. In the midst of separation we need to take a fresh look at God's Book and see that things are going to come together, lest looking at circumstances we dare to believe what we see rather than what God says. The day we start believing what we see around us is the day the enemy starts having control of us, for Satan has a way of manipulating circumstances; so if we live by circumstances, he can manipulate us. But if instead of living by what is seen in the newspaper, we dare to live by "every word that proceedeth out of the mouth of God" (Matthew 4:4), we can have peace in the midst of war and enjoy togetherness while there is separation all around us.

The Pre-fall Unity of All Things

Attempting to unfold these presumptions and to gain some understanding of the pre-fall unity of all things may very well call for the services of a trained philosopher, but that is not my area of expertise, and few of my readers would understand one even if I quoted him; so let's just review what we know of God's Word and use our sanctified imaginations to see what we can comprehend. Admittedly, we who have been born in sin and iniquity and have arrived on the scene long after the fall have great difficulty conceiving what it was like before the fall and the introduction of sin. We have a few hints, suggestions, and illuminations in the Word of God—just tiny bits of revelation—of how it must have been, but that is all. One of the first things we learn from the Bible is that there was perfect harmony in God, "Hear, O Israel; The Lord our God is one Lord" (Mark 12:29; Deuteronomy 6:4,5).

The Trinity has never been three Gods, and we create much difficulty, not only conceptually but experientially, when we allow ourselves to separate the Father, the Son, and the Holy Spirit into three distinct Persons who get along fine, but are three individuals. The Scripture teaches that there are not three Gods—"The Lord our God is one Lord"—there is but one God who has chosen to reveal Himself to us in three forms, and He has never been separated from Himself except for the brief interval at the cross when the Father turned His face from the Son. It was this separation between Father and Son that was the true agony of the cross; not the square Roman nails, nor the aftermath of the whipping post, nor the poisonous crown of thorns, nor the disjointing of arms and legs as the cross was dropped into the hole in the ground. The physical agony of the crucifixion was nothing to be compared with the separation in the Godhead occasioned by Christ's vicarious bearing of our sins in His own body on that cross. It was both the first and the last separation that the Godhead will ever know.

In this pre-fall unity of all things there was also perfect harmony among the heavenly creatures. The seraphim, cherubim, heavenly hosts, ministering spirits, and guardian angels lived and functioned together happily and harmoniously. There is no indication in the Scriptures to the contrary, while there is every evidence to the affirmative, that the state of heaven was peace, joy, harmony, happiness, completeness, fullness, and perfect unity.

Before the insurrection of Lucifer in the heavens there was only one will in all of creation. Myriads of angels had so completely submitted their wills to God that there was only one effective will extant—God's will. God said, "Let there be . . ." and there was, without reservation, hesitation, explanation, or committee action. This is the master key to eternity—the supremacy of God's will.

Before time began, nothing and no one challenged God's will. When time shall end, once again there will be no challenge to the will of God. Man, the earth-bound, time-space dimension creature, cannot conceive of the beauty and completeness of the unity and togetherness of eternity. It just doesn't fit anything to which he comfortably relates, for he lives in the midst of myriads of wills, but eternity has only one will—the will of the Father—and all, in surrendering to that one will, come into a togetherness and a unity that is fruitful and fulfilling both to them and to the purposes of God. Perfect harmony and peaceful happiness are the natural by-products of functioning obediently to one will.

It is patently obvious that something happened to disrupt the unity in heaven. Isaiah records that Lucifer, the anointed cherub that covered the Ark, began to exert a second will into eternity by saying, "*I will.*" This exercise of Lucifer's will was in direct competition with, and opposition to, the will of God. He cried, ". . . I will *ascend* into heaven, I will *exalt* my throne above the stars of God: I will *sit* also upon the mount of the congregation, in the sides of the north: I will *ascend above* the heights of the clouds; I will *be like* the most High" (Isaiah 14:13,14, italics added).

The moment Lucifer made this five-fold assertion of his will, the holiness and righteousness of eternity were blemished and tarnished. No longer was Lucifer content to be a part of God's place, authority, and position. Therefore, there came into the universe a second will, rising from the heart of Lucifer, the highest and most wonderful of all the created beings in the universe. Nothing and no one, short of God, was as great as he, but pride caused him to want to rise one step higher. Therefore, in addition to the voice of God, there was now a second voice saying, "I will!" Obviously this was rebellion, but far more important than the rebellion was the fact that there were two wills: the will of God, and the will of Lucifer; and that meant conflict.

At this exact point eternity was interrupted, and God introduced a parenthesis that we call time. The differentiation between time and eternity is not duration but disposition. Time is where there is more than one will; eternity is where all wills have become one. The quality of *eternity* is the fact that there is only one will, the will of God. The quality of *time* is that there is more than one will; this is the dividing factor.

Probably the shortest definition of sin is simply, "I will," and it makes no difference who speaks the words, for the moment there is an expression of any will in opposition to God's will there is sin! In his latest book, *The Invisible War,* Dr. Donald Grey Barnhouse writes, "The will of God is a line of truth and goodness that is unbending. It moves straight and with certainty across the universe of space, time, and thought. Any variation from that will of God, be it only in the slightest fraction of a degree, causes a tangent of separation and deviation—and that is sin."

So eternity was interrupted by the introduction of a second will. In the midst of the interruption God created man,

reformed the earth that seems to have been Lucifer's head-
quarters until his expulsion from heaven, and gave dominion over this recreated planet to Adam. It didn't take Satan
long to discover that God had given to His man what had
been denied the angels—the power of procreation. I like to
postulate that Satan's thought was, *I have not been able to
outvote God; I was able to bring only a small segment of
heaven's angels with me in my banishment, but if I had just a
few more on my side I might yet replace God.* Seeing man's
ability to reproduce himself, Satan made his subtle approach to entice man to surrender his will to Satan, rather
than to stay in the will of God, and this temptation was almost successful. But Adam did not say, "I vote with you,
Lucifer"; what Adam declared was, "I will," and then we
had three wills functioning in creation: God's will, Satan's
will, and Adam's will. In the course of time Adam and Eve
had a child named Cain, who rose up to express his own will
in the matter of how to worship, and then there were four
wills.

The curse of humanity is the continuous exercise of self-
will, and every time we manifest it, we deviate that much
farther from the will of the Father and get that much farther
from eternity. *Time* is a dimension of increasing evident
wills, and now we who are in the lengthening shadows of at
least the beginnings of the end are face-to-face with humanism, which deifies the singular will. In my earlier days in the
ministry it wasn't too difficult to convince individuals that
they were sinners by simply mentioning the exercise of their
self-will against God's revealed will, but today that doesn't
seem to mean anything to people. They have been trained
from their childhood to believe that the will of the individual is sacred. The emphasis is on doing what the individual

chooses to do, and yet this is the very philosophy that disrupted eternity, brought time into being, and produced the precise disunity that has cursed the period called time. If we had the capacity to see with the eyes of God, we would observe thousands times tens of thousands of self-wills being exercised on the face of the earth.

For years we have been taught that people are either servants of God or servants of the devil, but this is not at all consistent with the Scriptures. There probably are relatively few individuals who are out-and-out servants of the devil; most are servants of themselves. Satan doesn't have much voluntary submission to his will; everyone wants to exercise his own will, and far more people live in their own wills than live in the will of Satan. Frankly, the devil has quite a difficult time getting people to surrender their wills to him for any lengthy period of time, and about the time he succeeds in getting an individual to come under his will, God removes that person from the face of the earth, and Satan has to start over again with someone else.

The longer I live the worse this exercise of self-will seems to become. There was a day when American individuals conscientiously submitted their wills to the will of society, and law and order prevailed. We didn't even have locks on our cars, and very few locked their houses. But now amidst the projection of extreme humanism, which deifies the individual and declares that each should do as he wills—drink as you will, take drugs as you will, rob and steal what you need, act and function as you will—society is degenerating, and life as we have known it no longer exists. Furthermore, there seems to be nothing we can do through legislation or force to change it. Our officials are frustrated; they don't know how to correct the situation, for the moment they seem to control one small angle of this rebellion, there comes a new release of defiance against society, to say nothing of the insurrection against God and His will. If people in society ever get together again, and if all these multiple millions of wills ever become surrendered to one will, it will have to be by a divine act, not by any human exploit.

The Plan of Restoration

When Paul wrote, "That in the dispensation of the fulness of times he might gather together in one all things in Christ ..." (Ephesians 1:10), the Greek word he chose to use for "together" is *anakephalaiomai,* which has three distinct meanings. Primarily it signifies to restore, renew, and reduce to a former state, and the Vulgate Latin and Syriac versions of the New Testament render it this way. God has purposed to restore or reduce things to a former state where there was only one will extant—His will. Paul's use of this combination Greek word points to the restoration of all things, as the prophets spoke, for they consistently wrote about a tremendous restoration of things in the heavens and things on the earth. Today we have a segment of the Christian believers who still expect this, but, sadly, the majority of Christians long ago wrote off any possibility of a return to a theocracy. They declare that it just cannot be done, and if by this they mean there is no way man can do it, they are correct. But by the very use of this word we are challenged to believe that God intends to restore what sin has ruined and to renew the former relationship where His will prevails in heaven and earth. God is going to gather the fragmented pieces of human experience and renew them into a united whole where men and God, men and angels, and men and men are harmoniously flowing in God's perfect will. God has promised to reduce everything to what it was originally and bring it back to its prime.

This "gather together" Paul spoke of must also include the restoration and renovation of the universe—the new heavens and the new earth. Peter assured us that ". . . the heavens shall pass away with a great noise, and the elements shall melt with fervent heat . . ." (2 Peter 3:10), while in his vision on the isle of Patmos John said, "And I saw a new heaven and a new earth: for the first heaven and the first earth were passed away . . ." (Revelation 21:1). Not only will our lives be purged from every exercise of self-will; the very earth that has been polluted by rebellious men will be purged with fire and renewed and restored to its former relationship with heaven. It will be changed from what it now is to what it once was, and our planet will take its place in the perfect will of God.

While it is common among Christians to say, "I'm so looking forward to the coming of the Lord Jesus Christ so that all things can become new," we might be more accurate if we said that we're looking forward to all things becoming *old,* for God's purpose is to return everything to the old state of affairs where the divine will reigns supreme! The day must come where God breaks down the many multiple wills to where we stop merely singing, "He Is Lord," and start functioning obediently under His Lordship.

As touching the Church, Paul did not see this restored unity as totally futuristic. He wrote, "Endeavouring to keep the unity of the Spirit in the bond of peace. There is one body, and one Spirit, even as ye are called in one hope of your calling; One Lord, one faith, one baptism, One God and Father of all, who is above all, and through all, and in you all" (Ephesians 4:3–6). The Church is not challenged to produce this; we are told that there *is* one body, Spirit, hope, Lord, faith, baptism, and God. This unity—this oneness—has been produced by God's Spirit, and we are required to "make every effort to keep the unity of the Spirit . . ." (NIV). In *heaven* there is but one each of the above seven things, and on *earth* there is but one each of the seven listed things. There is one series of seven in heaven, and one series of seven on earth, and the series are identical. There is one Body in heaven, and the same Spirit is on earth. There is one Spirit in heaven, and the same Body is on earth. At least in these seven areas, all that shall be in heaven is now available on earth in miniscule quantity. The beginnings are here. The genesis is now. We can now come into that which will unite us, and when we get to heaven we'll be no stranger to it, for it will simply be more of the same, greatly enlarged and enhanced but not too different from what we've enjoyed of God here on the earth.

God in His grace has brought some of eternity into the dimension of time, so that when time ceases and we find ourselves completely in eternity we will not be lost, strange, or unfamiliar. We dare not forget that the big difference between time and eternity is in quality, not quantity, and the quality is "one will." The more our will is surrendered to the divine will, the more of eternity we can enter now. The New Testament teaches not that we look forward to eternal life, but that we now are participants in eternal life. John wrote, "This is the record, that God hath given to us eternal life, and this life is in his Son. He that hath the Son hath life; and he that hath not the Son of God hath not life" (1 John 5:11,12).

We come into a quality of eternal life because at the cross we surrendered our will to the will of God and declared that we would no longer walk in our way but in God's way. If the quality of sin is the exercise of the self-will, then the quality of salvation is the renunciation of that self-will in submission to the divine will. It is this change in governing wills that enables us to step into eternal life. However limited in quantity it may be, it is identical in quality to what we will enjoy throughout our stay in heaven with the Lord Jesus.

In sharing eternal life with us while we are still locked into time, and in assuring us that the same Body, Spirit, hope, Lord, faith, baptism, and Father that reside and preside in heaven are now present here on earth, God has given us a foretaste in order to create a taste for that eternal life. It speaks of a unity that is extremely difficult for us to comprehend because there seems to be a vast separation between heaven and earth in our experience. But all separation is on man's part, not on God's part. The Scriptures never speak of God's being reconciled to man; it is always man's being reconciled to God. God does not need to be reconciled to man because He never separated Himself from us, but we need to be reconciled to God because we withdrew from His will by the exercise of a self-will against God. God waits for man to approach Him, and the moment man begins to submit his will to the divine will, he starts to become part of the "together" Paul is talking about. We are placed "in Christ," and this Christ is now managing the affairs of life to bring into realization what is now but a visualization. What now requires the eye of faith shall someday become an exposed reality that all may see.

Richard Francis Weymouth, in his *New Testament in Modern Speech,* translates this passage, "... He made known to us the secret of His will. And this is in harmony with God's merciful purpose for the government of the

world when the times are ripe for it—the purpose which He
has cherished in His own mind of restoring the whole creation to find its one Head in Christ; yes, things in heaven and
things on earth, to find their one Head in Him" (Ephesians
1:9,10). This is God's ultimate purpose.

The Proportion of That Restoration

I stated that Paul's word *anakephalaiomai* had three distinct meanings, but I have so far confined its interpretation
to the concept of restoring, renewing, and reducing to a former state. But scholars of the Greek language tell us that this
word is also used to recapitulate or sum up the heads of a
discourse, very much as the heading separating this para-
graph from the preceding one briefly summarizes what is
going to follow. Its purpose is to help you follow as we
change the thought from "a"to "b." This word Paul used,
and which we translate "gather together," speaks of Christ's
being the subtitle, the heading of all things. Christ is God's
headline of what has been and is the subtitle of all that shall
be. All the promises and blessings of the covenants of the
Bible are captioned in Jesus Christ. All the prophecies and
promises of the Old Testament are revealed in Jesus, for
". . . the testimony of Jesus is the spirit of prophecy" (Revelation 19:10). All of the types and shadows, the sacrifices and
ceremonies of the former dispensation, are fulfilled and dis-
played in the Lord Jesus. Even the fullness of the New Testament promises find their title in Him. Jesus is God's headline! Everything is capsulized in Him. Little wonder, then,
Paul cried out, "That I may know him . . ." (Philippians
3:10), for Christ is the summation of all of God's revelation
to man. All things are recapitulated or subtitled in Him.

These same Greek scholars tell us that in classical Greek

anakephalaiomai is sometimes used for the collection of numbers into one sum total. It is the answer to the listed column of figures, which the Greeks always put at the top of the column rather than at the bottom as we commonly do. Christ is not only the sum of all things; He is also the head of all. Christ is the sum total of angels and men. He is the aggregate of all human history. He is the accumulation of everything in heaven, and He is *above* all. Jesus Christ is the final answer.

The teaching of this passage is that just as a paper dollar stands for four quarters, ten dimes, or one hundred pennies, so Christ stands as the summation of all things in heaven and all things upon the earth. He sums them all up; He brings them all into one. All things are included in Him; they are complete in Him; they are consummated in Him. Never lose sight of the fact that Jesus Christ is the only Person who ever lived for whom such a claim has been made. We may declare that a movement has been summed up in a man—as we equate Martin Luther with Lutheranism—and we may write a summation of a period of history in a person—as George Washington and the American Revolution—but no man ever lived of whom it was seriously claimed that he summed up *all* things. Yet everything is summed up in Christ Jesus.

Jesus sums up *all truth*. He does not have a monopoly on truth—He *is* the Truth, for He Himself declared, "I am... the truth . . ." (John 14:6). Many religions of the world have correct facts, good philosophies, and high ideals, but Jesus is the *truth*. He is God's last word, and He is never a back number; He is never out of date. Jesus is as current in our decade of the atom as He was in Martin Luther's day when they were trying to find their way out of the Dark Ages. Jesus is the summation of all truth.

Furthermore, Jesus sums up *all humanity.* He is not simply prophet and Messiah; He is the Son of Man. He is more than the representative man; He is the all-inclusive, universal Man. He was God's man to take the place of all humanity on Calvary's cross. In calling Christ "the last Adam" and "the second man" (1 Corinthians 15:45,47), Paul establishes that the entire lineage of Adam died in Christ Jesus, and He began a totally new lineage called "the second man." Christ wiped the slate clean of one lineage and started an entirely new dynasty of "sons of God."All humanity has its roots, its beginnings, in Christ Jesus. He sums it all up.

Equally, Jesus sums up *all saving and redeeming grace.* If Jesus does not save the world, nobody else can. Sin is not a violation of the written Word of God—the Bible. If it were, then there would be no sin where there was no written law of God. Sin existed long before the Bible was written. Sin is transgression in an individual's heart; it is a breaking of the law of his own life that was God given; it is, remember, the exercise of the self-will against God's will, whether that will is known through reading the written page or through an inner awareness of the principles of life. The Bible did not come to make men sinners, but to reveal that they were sinners, and to reveal a Saviour. When we find Jesus we find salvation, not because of what we think, or even what we believe about Him, but because we find Him, and *He* is the Saviour of the world. The issue dare never become "my doctrine versus your doctrine," for your doctrine cannot save you, and my doctrine cannot save me. It's not our doctrine, our views, our attitudes, our pet Scripture verses that we quote; Jesus is the Saviour. All saving and redeeming grace is wrapped up in One—that Man Christ Jesus!

The stated purpose of togetherness, at least in its ultimate purpose, is to get everything back into its original state, harmoniously under Christ. By virtue of divine grace Christ offers a friendship between elect angels and elect men—not a friendship that can be or shall be, but one that is now available where the angels function as ". . . ministering spirits, sent forth to minister for them who shall be heirs of salvation" (Hebrews 1:14). By the vicariousness of Calvary Christ brought man and God together in a friendly relationship that is practical and personal. Jesus told His disciples, "Henceforth I call you not servants . . . but I have called you friends . . ." (John 15:15). We can come into a restored relationship whereby man and God enjoy the affability of friendship. Furthermore, by uniting us into a family Christ restored fellowship between men, in spite of great cultural, educational, and social differences. In Christ we find a common denominator for fellowship that ignores and transcends our human differences.

There even seems to be a uniting of the saints in heaven with the saints on earth, for in Ephesians 3:15 Paul speaks of "the whole family in heaven and earth" being named after Jesus. The Greek word Paul uses for "family" is *patria,* which speaks of parental descent, that is, a group of families, a whole race, or an entire nation. Ken Taylor translates this verse, ". . . the Father of all the great family of God—some of them already in heaven and some down here on earth" (Ephesians 3:15 TLB). God has but one family, and its differences are geographical, not generic. That the heavenly branch of the family is concerned with and is observing the earthly branch of the family seems to be suggested in Hebrews 12:1, which speaks of the great saints of chapter 11 as "a great cloud of witnesses" who surround us. They're looking on, seeking to encourage us to continue in the race, and their worship in the heavens is mingled with our worship on the earth. It is all embryonic now, but it will be enlarged as God gets everything together more and more.

Gathering Together Is Not Equatable With Universalism

This verse does not teach universalism or the ultimate reconciliation of all things, whereby some teachers declare that even the devil himself will be reconciled with God eventually. Such teachers expect all men to be restored to heaven whether they have embraced the cross and the Christ or not. The fundamental basis for their doctrine is Paul's consistent use of the word *all,* which they understand to mean all shall be saved. In the Ephesians volume of the *Tyndale New Testament Commentaries* Francis Foulkes writes: "This verse has been used as the keystone of the doctrine of 'universalism,' that all men shall be saved in the end. It does imply that in the end everything and every being in existence will be under His *authority,* but it is dangerous to press a doctrine from a verse without regard for the balance of the evidence of Scripture, as a whole, and, in this case, without respect for the solemn presentation from one end of Scripture to the other of the alternatives of life and death dependent on the acceptance or rejection of God's salvation."

Paul limits this "together in one" to things "in heaven, and which are on earth" but *not* things in hell. We dare not try to make God reconcile things He has not promised to reconcile. The things in heaven and the things on earth are going to get together in Christ, but the things in hell will never be reconciled either to the redeemed or to their Redeemer.

It helps us understand this better when we realize that Paul is speaking about universal dominion, not universal salvation. The day will come when all things shall be under the dominion of God, even the things in hell, for actually it is not the devil's hell; it is God's hell.

The *Wesleyan Bible Commentary* suggests that "ultimately all things, willfully rebellious men excluded, will be redeemed and reunited in the body of Christ and thus He will be the head of all things. This is the Christian view of the goal of all history. How different is this verse from that of the contemporary philosopher Bertrand Russell, who thinks that all things 'must inevitably be buried beneath the debris of a universe in ruins.' "

"All things must inevitably be buried beneath the debris of a universe in ruins" is not only Bertrand Russell's view, but is also the inner fear of many politicians, economists, and world leaders. The reign of terrorism, the destruction of runaway inflation, the constant warfare on our planet, and the continuing breakdown of the moral fiber of our people seem to lead to the same conclusion. But God is not yet through with this world. When men get desperate enough to give Him a chance to rule, righteousness and peace shall again dominate mankind. We Christians can relax and rejoice in God, for we have been allowed to read the last chapter of the book. As J. B. Phillips translates these verses, "For God has allowed us to know the secret of his plan, and it is this: he purposed long ago in his sovereign will that all human history will be consummated in Christ, that everything that exists in Heaven or earth should find its perfection and fulfilment in him" (Ephesians 1:9,10).

The Book that describes this final consummation declares that the day is coming when a mighty angel will stand upon the earth "and sware by him that liveth for ever and ever, who created heaven, and the things that therein are, and the earth, and the things that therein are, and the sea, and the things which are therein, that *there should be time no longer*" (Revelation 10:6, italics added). Time shall be no more! Why? Because there will be a point when there will only be *one will,* and at whatever point all wills are again surrendered to the divine will, there will be no need for time; we'll go right back into eternity. I would like to be able to believe that at that point all will be converted and Christianized, but that is not what it says. What it does declare is that there will be a point where all wills come back into subjection to the will of Almighty God. The rebels who will not surrender to His love will be placed in God's prison and will not have an opportunity to exercise a self-will against God, while the saints who have surrendered voluntarily to God will join Him in the glories that have been prepared for them; but there will only be one will—God's will! Then the fullness of eternal life will begin to flow, for this is God's ultimate purpose in getting all things together.

Fortunately, however, the process of this togetherness is already at work in the lives of the redeemed. They are *now* partakers of the very life of God through Jesus Christ. They have been "quickened together with Christ" (Ephesians 2:5).

Section II

God's Process for Getting Us Together

[God] ... hath quickened us together with Christ, (by grace ye are saved;) And hath raised us up together, and made us sit together in heavenly places in Christ Jesus.

Ephesians 2:5,6

4

Quickened Together With Christ

Quite some years ago during my first visit to Australia my host took me to the construction site of the now-famous Sydney Opera House. In a temporary building they had a scale model of what the completed building was to look like, plus many displays explaining the process they had gone through to get to their present stage of construction. These visual presentations explained that the design for this building was chosen from many plans submitted by hundreds of competing architects, but after the contract was awarded, the architect discovered to his dismay that he could not successfully engineer the unique roof design he had drawn. He had succeeded in building the scale model that had fired the imagination of the planning committee, but, try as he would, he could not engineer the actual plans for the construction of the unique opera house. After lengthy delays and repeated costly failures, he was removed from the project, and the contract was awarded to another architect, who was instructed to keep the original concept but to develop a way to construct it. The fact that the building now stands in Sydney's harbor, with its multiple roofs giving the appearance of schooners with sails billowing in a full wind, gives evidence that the second builder was able to engineer

what the first man was able only to design. The original
winner of the competition was able to conceive a magnificent plan, but he was unable to construct the building.

Although this may be most unusual in architectural cir-
cles, it is quite consistent with many of our experiences in
life, for most of us have learned that our anticipative per-
ception far exceeds our ability to perform. But this is never
true with our God. He has never conceived anything He was
unable to construct, nor has He ever planned anything that
He could not perform. Paul was assured of this, for he wrote,
"Being confident of this very thing, that he which hath
begun a good work in you will perform it until the day of
Jesus Christ" (Philippians 1:6).

Therefore, when we read in chapter 1 of Ephesians that
God's ultimate purpose is to bring all things together in and
under Christ Jesus, we may be well assured that He has already designed a process that will implement His purpose.
This process is unveiled in the second chapter of Ephesians
where Paul explains that God has done three things in the
lives of the believers to make it possible for them to get together in Christ Jesus.

Quickened With Christ

God has *quickened* us together with Christ, *raised* us up
together with Christ, and He has *seated* us together with
Christ. We have been revived, raised, and we now reign as
regents with Christ Jesus. We live by His life, walk in His
life, and reign through His life. God's process for getting us
together is to make us partners with Christ in everything
from the cross to the crown.

"[God] even when we were dead in sins, hath quickened

us together with Christ, (by grace ye are saved)" (Ephesians
2:5). The Greek word which we have translated "quickened" is *sunzoopoieo,* which actually means "to (re-)vi-
talize with, to reanimate conjointly, to make alive with, or
to quicken with." The New International Version simply
translates this verse, "[God] ... made us alive with Christ
even when we were dead in transgressions ..." (Ephesians
2:5).

That God made man alive in the beginning is incontestable, for the account of man's creation declares that "the
Lord God formed man out of the dust of the ground, and
breathed into his nostrils the breath of life; and man became
a living soul" (Genesis 2:7). Man's life is different in character from every other living thing on this earth in that it came
as an impartation of the very life of God. Adam possessed
more than animal life; he was a recipient of divine life—he
had a soul in addition to his body. He was united together
with God not only in purpose and position, but as sharer of
a common life. He shared the life of God as surely as I share
the life of my mother and father.

It was certainly God's provision that this life be perpetuated in the human race, but sin entered and the consequences of sin—death—replaced that divine life. God had
stated, "... in the day that thou eatest thereof thou shalt
surely die" (Genesis 2:17). Obviously Adam did not die bio-
logically the day he disobeyed God, for he lived to the age of
930 years (*see* Genesis 5:5) and became the progenitor of the
human race. But the very day Adam and Eve chose their
own will over the revealed will of God, Adam lost that glorious divine life that had been breathed into him, and were it
not for the special sacrificial provision God made for Adam

that day in the garden, Adam would have been forever cut off from access to God.

Sin separated man from everything with which God had united him. Sin forced Adam's expulsion from the garden of Eden, prohibited his access to the tree of life, and greatly restricted his fellowship with God. The results of sin are as devastating in our twentieth century as they were back in the days of Adam and Eve. No amount of education, enlightenment, or experience has enabled mankind to erase or eradicate the consequences of sin. Conversely, man spends most of his time and energies combating these very consequences.

Sin marred and scarred man's relationship with God. The invigorating walks and talks with God in Eden's garden were forfeited forever. Adam was not severed from God's love or His provision, but he was permanently separated from God's presence. Even today men are still separated from God's presence because of sin. A knowledge of God may pervade our conscious mind, and the love of God protects our daily life, but man, still in his sin, cannot come into the presence of God. Not only may he not come into God's presence, but it is rare that he is even aware of the presence of God. Whereas man was originally made for fellowship and communion with God, his sin separated him from God, thereby restricting his fellowship to other sinful human creatures.

It is somewhat like the doctors, lawyers, and politicians who fled from Vietnam to immigrate to America but found that their training and experience are unacceptable here. So they took very menial jobs and contented themselves with living lives very much beneath the level of life that they were used to. They were both born and trained to a higher station in life, but war destroyed that for them once and for all. At a far greater contrast, sin destroyed man's purpose of being, and it has forever restricted man to a level of life barely above that of the animal kingdom.

As penalizing as these consequences of sin may be, the ultimate end of sin is death. Sin killed what God created! Sin brought a curse on the earth, violence to earth's creatures, and death to man who was created to rule in authority over all of God's creation. Sin has destroyed man's access to the tree of life, has massacred his innocence and purity, and has assassinated his physical life.

Death cannot have fellowship with life any more than light can have communion with darkness, so before God could bring us together with Himself in Jesus, He had to bring us from death to life, and this He did through the work of Calvary's cross. Christ not only died as God's lamb, paying the ultimate penalty for sin, but He died in our place, as our substitute. Christ not only died *for* us, but we died *in* Christ. As surely as He vicariously bore our sins, we victoriously share His death.

The workings of death were irreversible, but the finality of death was replaceable. God replaced death with life! Those who came to Christ's tomb to embalm His dead body soon discovered that God had exchanged life for death. They were questioned by the angels, ". . . Why seek ye the living among the dead? He is not here, but is risen . . ." (Luke 24:5,6). What God did in Jesus He does in us in order that we may get together again. Paul told the Christians in Colossae, "And you, being dead in your sins and the uncircumcision of your flesh, hath he quickened together with him, having forgiven you all trespasses" (Colossians 2:13). Here again, Paul uses the combined Greek word *sunzoopoieo,* which means "made alive with." We are not quickened apart from Christ Jesus; we become a part of Christ's quickening. It is not a separate life, but the same life that brought Christ from the grave, that lifts us from the death of sin, for we are assured that "... if the Spirit of him that raised up Jesus from the dead dwell in you, he that raised up Christ from the dead shall also quicken your mortal bodies by his Spirit that dwelleth in you" (Romans 8:11). Paul places the action in the present rather than in the future, for it is our mortal, not our immortal, body that is quickened.

The Spirit who brought Christ from death to life is now operative in the Church to bring individuals from the death of sin to the life of the Spirit. God is now quickening His saints, and He is giving the very same life He gave to His Son in order to reestablish fellowship at the highest possible level, for life can only truly fellowship life of the same kind. A dog fellowships a dog, and a frog fellowships a frog, but it would be a stretch of the metaphor to suggest that a dog could fellowship a frog. Therefore, God has chosen to impart the very same Spirit to us who was imparted at the resurrection of Jesus Christ, so that we would not only have life but would have life of the same kind, thereby restoring a fundamental basis for fellowship and communion with God.

Since this quickening is an action of God's eternal Spirit, which Christ declares was His Spirit whom He promised to send to His disciples, it is not so much quickened persons who live as it is Christ who lives in and through them. We are not so much given life and then told to live it as it is that we receive life and allow that life to live through us. A more intimate basis for fellowship could not have been found.

Alive Unto God

"Alive unto God" (Romans 6:11); "and you hath he quickened, who were dead in trespasses and sins" (Ephesians 2:1). What a splendid summation of the complex plan of salvation. From *God's side* the problem was sin, the process was substitution, and the purpose was sonship. From *man's side* the problem was untimely death, the process was reckoning, and the purpose was unity with God. God revoked the power of sin, restored the status of sonship, and once again shared His divine life with mankind. This renewed life reestablishes the togetherness that man had forfeited.

We have received life because God "hath quickened us together with Christ" (Ephesians 2:5), but it is not sufficient to have received life; we must maintain that life. In the natural, life is received by action of our parents wholly outside of ourselves, but from the moment of our birth onward the maintenance of that life was dependent upon forces within us. Outer actions contributed, but the life was within us as growing children. Similarly, the initial source of spiritual life is God, and it is imparted by virtue of forces wholly outside ourselves, but the maintenance of that life becomes dependent upon us. Although God will supply the means, we must apply them, or the life He has imparted will soon be depleted.

"Lord Quicken Me"

Hezekiah, the godly king of Judah, lay upon his sickbed chafing over the message of the prophet Isaiah that death was imminent and that he should set his house in order. In his grief Hezekiah pleaded with God for an extension of his life. God was entreated by that prayer, and Isaiah was sent back to the king with the message that God was extending his days here on the earth. Many Bible scholars think that it was during this extension that Hezekiah collected the sundry prayers, praises, and professions of obedience that are arranged in an alphabetic acrostic forming Psalm 119. While the overriding theme of this Psalm is the Word of God (evident by the fact that God's Word is mentioned in every verse), the secondary theme that forms somewhat of a counterpoint to the melody is "quicken me." The Hebrew word used for "quicken" is *chayah,* which occurs fifteen times in this Psalm, and every time the word appears it is in the third conjugation—the piel voice—which denotes action. The Hebrew language conjugates its verbs seven ways, and the sense of the verb greatly varies the meaning of the word. To illustrate this, consider the Hebrew word *qatal,* which means "kill." If it is in its first conjugation, we would translate it, "He killed." If it is in the second conjugation it would be translated, "He was killed," but if it appears in the third conjugation (the piel voice), it would be translated, "He killed violently." Consistently through Psalm 119 the cry is for extreme action: "Lord, quicken me violently, intravenously feed me, overmaster me with life."

This Psalm is not the only place in the Old Testament where *chayah* is used. Thirteen times it is translated, "save alive," six times it is translated, "revive," and five times it is translated as, "keep alive." It is the very word Abraham used when asking Sarah to say that she was his sister rather than his wife. He said, "They will kill me, but they will save thee alive" (Genesis 12:12).

It is not by accident, then, that the king whose life span had been extended by God's prophetic word, nine times in this one Psalm wrote, "Quicken me according to thy word" (*see* verses 25,37,40,50,88,93,107,149,154).

"Quicken Me" Is a Plea

This cry for a repeated quickening should be on the lips of all of God's redeemed. It would be better never to have experienced life than to have received it and then lost it. Peter put it this way: "For it had been better for them not to have known the way of righteousness, than, after they have known it, to turn from the holy commandment delivered unto them" (2 Peter 2:21). One of the heartaches experienced by conscientious pastors is the percentage of born-again believers who do not seem to maintain life. They may well be rescued from hell and even assured of a place in heaven, but they are lifeless, listless, and unresponsive to things spiritual. They may know doctrine, but they do not know God. They may fellowship other believers, but they do not fellowship God. They seem totally unaware of the spirit world and would likely expect to drop dead if an angel appeared unto them.

We have not merely been redeemed from sin; we have been restored to life. Now we must learn to live that life and to perpetuate it. What some Christians fail to realize is that whenever life ebbs, we become subject to disease and sickness. My oldest daughter is a nurse, and she attests that the state of the art of medicine and surgery is so high that if an individual gets medical attention sufficiently early, he will probably be cured of his ailment. However, in the treatment, whether by surgery or medicine, it often becomes necessary to lower the life forces almost to the point of "the valley of the shadow of death," as in anesthetizing the patient before surgery. While the bodily forces are at such a low ebb, the body's resistance to infection is often so weak that a simple infection that would not have been sufficient to cause the loss of one day of work when the patient was in normal health might kill him before the infection was even discovered. It is not so much the force of the infection from without our body but the strength of the resistance within the body that determines health or sickness. Similarly, it is not the strength of the demonic attack but the power of the Spirit within the believer that determines the result of the temptation or assault. We have been assured that "... greater is he that is in you, than he that is in the world" (1 John 4:4). Life is God's antidote to death, but life must be replenished as it is used.

Christians sometimes fail to realize that life is exhausted not only by living it, but by sharing it. When Jesus was enroute to Jericho, a little woman with an issue of blood sought His healing power, but being unable to attract His attention, she merely pressed through the mobbing throng of the entourage and touched the hem of Christ's garment. Instantly she was healed, and Jesus turned to His disciples and said, "Somebody hath touched me: for I perceive that virtue is gone out of me" (Luke 8:46). The woman fearfully confessed, and we may well assume that the disciples dutifully protested, but Jesus did not condemn the woman; He merely expressed His awareness that divine energy had been transferred from Him to her. The Greek word Jesus used, and which we have translated as "virtue," is *dunamis*—the very same word that Christ used just before His ascension in promising, "But ye shall receive power, [*dunamis*], after that the Holy Ghost is come upon you ..." (Acts 1:8). If this *dunamis*—this divine power— was expendable in the life of

Jesus, how much more is it exhaustible in us. When we minister to another, assuming that they receive something more than words from us, we are depleted by the same measure of divine energy that they receive. How imperative it is, then, that we learn how to replenish our supply, for we will soon exhaust our original provision and have to function in the memory of what once was instead of in the reality of what now is.

While it is true that Jesus prayed all night before major ministries, the Gospels also record that He often prayed throughout the night *after* a major ministry. He went into the presence of the Father to receive power, and then, having expended that power upon the needy, He returned for a fresh supply. One of the major causes of "burn out" in the ministry is the failure to maintain a fresh flow of divine life. Hezekiah's plea needs to become the plea of every Christian worker: "Lord, quicken me according to thy word."

"Quicken Me" Is a Promise

The cry "Quicken me *according to thy word*" is more than a plea of need; it is the pleading of a promise. God said it, so that settles it; please send it! Happy is the Christian who has learned to plead a promise rather than a need, for God answers His Word, not merely human need. When we have the authority of God's Word to stand upon, we pray effectually and according to God's will. "And this is the confidence that we have in him, that, if we ask any thing according to his will, he heareth us: and if we know that he hear us, whatsoever we ask, we know that we have the petitions that we desired of him" (1 John 5:14,15).

Has God actually promised us this life? Check the record! "And this is the record, that God hath given to us eternal life, and this life is in his Son. He that hath the Son hath life; and he that hath not the Son of God hath not life" (1 John, 5:11,12). God promised the life, placed it in His Son, and then sent that Son to dwell among men. While living with them, Jesus, who declared ". . . I am . . . the life . . ." (John 14:6), also added, ". . . I am come that they might have life, and that they might have it more abundantly" (John 10:10). Jesus the source became Jesus the supplier, and He offered that supply in three measures: "life," "more life," and "abundant life." He pledges an availability of eternal life in our time-space dimension.

Although Jesus remained on our planet only about thirty-three years, before He left He promised that He would send "another Comforter" (John 14:16), using the Greek word *paraclete* meaning "one called alongside to help." What Christ had been to them, this "other Comforter" would become to them. In seeking to further define this *Comforter*, Jesus said, "But when the Comforter is come, whom I will send unto you from the Father, even the Spirit of truth, which proceedeth from the Father, he shall testify of me" (John 15:26). In the book of Romans this "Spirit of truth" is called "the Spirit of life in Christ Jesus" (Romans 8:2). God put this quickening life in His Son, and the Son imparted this Spirit of Life to the believers. There should be no doubt that God has promised to "quicken me according to thy word."

"Quicken Me" Is a Provision

Nine times Psalm 119 follows this plea for quickening, with the qualifying phrase ". . . according to thy word." While this is certainly a promise, it is more than that; it is equally a provision. "Lord, quicken me through the me-

diacy of Thy Word." "Quicken me according to the operation of Thy Word." God not only promised a quickening
life; He provided it! While the ultimate source is in God's
Son, our access to the source is through God's Word. We do
ourselves a great disservice when we artifically separate the
Spirit of God from the Word of God. While we may want
them to function unilaterally, God has purposed that they
function unitedly. The Spirit and the Word agree, and when
they do not harmonize, we are listening to the wrong spirit
source, for God cannot contradict Himself.

In the wilderness God daily fed a multitude of people, es-
timated by Adam Clarke to exceed 4.5 million people. The
method of this provision was, "when the dew fell upoon the
camp in the night, the manna fell upon it" (Numbers 11:9).
No dew—no manna. Dew, in the Old Testament, is one of
the many types of the Holy Spirit (*see* Hosea 14:5). If the
manna was a type of the living Word of God, and Jesus said
that He was that manna (*see* John 6:48–51), then it is when
the Word rests upon the Spirit, that it gives life to us. The
Word without the Spirit can be not only dry but deadly, for
"the letter killeth, but the Spirit giveth life"(2 Corinthians
3:6). It is not the Scripture that is quoted but the Scripture
that is quickened by the Spirit that brings life. It is when the
Spirit causes the Bible to speak in very personal terms to our
life that we are revitalized and made alive. No dew—no
manna; no Spirit—no life!

We need to get into God's Word and get that Word into
us to remain alive. It takes the discipline of reading to get us
into the Word, but it requires the direction of the Spirit to
get that Word into us. When our action and His action com-
bine, we feast on heavenly manna called "angels' food" (*see*
Psalms 78:25). We, as all before us, are sustained by the

Word of God. Even Jesus realized this, for He told the tempter, "... Man shall not live by bread alone, but by every word that proceedeth out of the mouth of God" (Matthew 4:4). If that was Christ's source to sustain life, then it will work for us as well.

Recently I flew to Denmark to preach a major camp meeting there. I arrived in a state of spiritual depletion and physical exhaustion. Furthermore, I was emotionally hurting, for my brothers had buried my mother while I was flying across the ocean. I told the Lord that I had wasted His money in flying over to Denmark, for I didn't feel that I had anything to say to these Christians, and that even if God should give me a word, I didn't have the strength or emotional stamina to express it. God spoke to my spirit and asked me how He usually quickens me. Immediately I quoted from this Psalm 119, saying, "You quicken me according to Your Word, Lord."

"Then get into My Word," He replied.

"But, Lord, I have been," I answered. "I have already preached more than a hundred times this year, and I have written a book based on the sixty-eighth psalm. Furthermore, I have been teaching regularly in the Fountain Gate Bible school. How much more time could I spend in Your Word?"

"But son," He answered, *"all of that time in the Word has been for ministry to others. Get into the Word for ministry to yourself."*

Then I realized that my weakened condition had been brought about because although I had gathered much manna to serve to others, I had not been eating that manna for myself.

Since I had brought a gift of The Chronological Bible

along with me, I opened it and began to read at Genesis. I read until it was my turn to preach, and then I returned to my room after the service and read some more. Inasmuch as I did not understand Danish, which was spoken in the services, and since my interpreter preferred not to interpret anything but my preaching, I didn't attend any service in which I was not a participant. Instead, I stayed in my room and read the Bible. It was summer in Denmark, and they were experiencing only three hours of "darkness," which was actually nothing more than dusk since I could always see the bay about three miles away; so I read late into the nights. If after going to bed I found myself wakeful, I read the Bible, and it began to feed and strengthen me gloriously. The more it strengthened me the more I wanted to read it. During the twelve days I was in Denmark, I read the entire Bible through, and as I prepared to return home, I found myself stronger physically, emotionally, and spiritually than when I had arrived in that country. The Lord quickened me according to His Word.

"Quicken Me" Has a Purpose

The last time the word *chayah* (quicken) appears in Psalm 119 is in verse 175, where it is translated, "Let my soul live, and it shall praise thee." The ultimate purpose of being quickened, or being reanimated, with Christ Jesus is that we will return to the intimate relationship with God that inspires praise and worship. Man was made to praise the Lord, and worship is fundamentally love responding to love. When the relationship is right, worship is natural. While love is being received, it redounds back to God. But praise and worship cannot proceed from one who has severed his intimate relationship with God. "The dead praise not the

Lord," the psalmist cried (Psalms 115:17). It is only out of life that praise can flow, and abundant praise requires abundant life.

The spiritual life of an individual or a local congregation can be measured by the praise level and the worship response. All response to God must come out of relationship with God, and that "togetherness" requires a sameness of life. God is worshiped in divine life, not human animation. "Let me live," Hezekiah cried, "and I shall praise Thee." Dare our cry be anything less?

"It is the spirit that quickeneth; the flesh profiteth nothing ..." Jesus said in John 6:63. God's Spirit, acting through God's Word and upon God's children, becomes a life-giving force that brings us into the same eternal life that Jesus shares. Being partakers together with His life enables us to be sharers in all that life brings to Him, including resurrection power.

5

Raised Up Together With Christ

For centuries story writers have delighted in telling about an individual who was buried and later, for any one of a number of reasons, the body was exhumed only to discover that the person had come to life after burial but had been unable to get out of the casket and the grave. Whether or not such a happening has ever been verified, it forms a plot that appeals strongly to our imagination.

That God did not merely give life to His Son and then leave Him in the grave to fend for Himself is shown in Paul's statement, "And hath raised us up together . . ." (Ephesians 2:6). God both reanimated Christ in the tomb and released Him from the tomb.

The Persuasion of Christ's Resurrection

There were no eyewitnesses to the resurrection of Jesus. No mortal saw the divine power of God enter the tomb of Joseph of Arimathea and energize the lifeless body that had served our Lord Jesus Christ during His days here on earth. None of the disciples watched as Jesus left the grave clothes in which He had been wrapped and triumphantly walked through the doorway, which had been opened by angelic action. No, the story of the resurrection is not an eyewitness account; it is, more accurately, the report of those who discovered what had already happened.

But the lack of eyewitnesses to the actual event does not weaken the reality of the happening. We have the testimony of those disciples who saw the empty tomb, the word of the angels who declared that Christ was not among the dead but was risen as He had predicted, and we have the further testimony of Mary, who talked with the risen Lord. Even the soldiers who had been posted to guard the tomb gave testimony to the resurrection of Jesus. The empty tomb, the unwrapped but empty grave clothes, the absence of a corpse, and the repeated appearance of the living Christ to His disciples and many others clearly attest to the literal, bodily resurrection of the Lord.

The Roman executioners certified His death, and the testimony that a soldier's sword thrust to Christ's rib cage released blood and water is sufficient evidence of death to the medical profession. So Christ did not merely swoon and later revive in the cool tomb. The behavior of Christ after the resurrection would in itself refute the swoon theory, for He did not behave as a man who had undergone a beating and crucifixion just a few days before. He always appeared and functioned in full strength as though nothing had happened at all.

For Christian believers none of the above "proofs" of the resurrection of Jesus is needed. The fact that the Bible clearly and repeatedly declares that Christ rose from the dead by the manifested power of God is more than sufficient. As further proof, however, we have to admit that the disciples and the Christians of that day firmly believed in Christ's resurrection, for they were transformed by His presence. It was the reality of the resurrection that gave them boldness in the face of grave persecution and drove them on to great missionary enterprise even in the face of danger and obstacles. It was because of their belief in and their preaching of the resurrection of Jesus Christ that thousands of them were martyred, but they were so convinced of the reality of the resurrection that they would not recant their faith even to save their lives.

There will always be skeptics who say it didn't happen, because they cannot explain how God did it, but there is probably no event in history that has more verification than the resurrection of Christ Jesus. God raised Christ from the dead, and this event has become the cornerstone of our faith.

The Peculiarity of Christ's Resurrection

While returning from the dead has been a fantasy of men from the beginning of time, it had been a fact long before God raised Christ from the dead. In the Old Testament when Elijah became aware that the son of the woman who had befriended him was dead, he pleaded with God for a resurrection, and the boy came to life again (*see* 1 Kings 17:17–23), and many years later the protegé of this great prophet, Elisha, also raised from the dead the Shunammite's son (*see* 2 Kings 4:18–37). Much later, after Elisha had been buried for many years, a soldier killed in the heat of a battle was hastily thrown into Elisha's tomb, and the moment that dead man touched the bones of Elisha, he came to life and rejoined the battle (*see* 2 Kings 13:21). So coming back from the dead was not a New Testament exclusive.

Furthermore, Jesus was not the first person in the New Testament to come back from the dead, for He, Himself, broke up the funeral at Nain by restoring a mother's son to life, and He had raised Lazarus from the dead just a short time before the crucifixion. No, Jesus was not the first person to rise from the dead, but He was the first person to come back from the grave permanently. All others eventually died a second time and now await the final resurrection, but Christ Jesus rose as the "first fruits of them that slept" (*see* 1 Corinthians 15:20). He was the first to exchange mortality for immortality. He came from the tomb clothed in a glorified body that was a prototype of the glorious spiritual body God had prepared for all of His saints. Christ was the first person to conquer death, hell, and the grave. All others had merely been granted a reprieve. In a sense we might say that Christ was God's "test run" that proved the feasibility of the plan of the resurrection, and He proved that it works marvelously!

The Power of Christ's Resurrection

In the first chapter of Ephesians Paul had prayed that "the eyes of your understanding being enlightened; that ye may know . . . what is the exceeding greatness of his power to us-ward who believe, according to the working of his mighty power, which he wrought in Christ, when he raised him from the dead, and set him at his own right hand in the heavenly places" (Ephesians 1:18–20). In the Old Testament the event that became the measurement of the power of God was the passage of the children of Israel through the parted Red Sea, but in the New Testament God's power is measured by the resurrection of Christ from the dead.

Our finite minds cannot conceive of the nature of the power that could raise the dead, giving a different form of life and body than that which went into the grave, nor can we devise any gauge whereby we can measure the amount of power that it would take. Still Paul cried, "That I may know him and the power of his resurrection . . . if by any means I might attain unto the resurrection of the dead" (Philippians 3:10,11). While we may not understand the nature of the magnitude of God's resurrection power, we yearn to have it operating in our own lives.

We have been amply assured of the availability of this resurrection life, and the entire New Testament assures us that since Christ lives, we shall live also (*see* John 14:19). Because of this, Paul assured the believers in Thessalonica, "I would not have you to be ignorant, brethren, concerning them which are asleep, that ye sorrow not, even as others who have no hope. For if we believe that Jesus died and rose again, even so them also which sleep in Jesus will God bring with him" (1 Thessalonians 4:13,14). It is the resurrection of Jesus Christ and the promise of our subsequent resurrection that brings comfort to Christian mourners.

The Parallel to Christ's Resurrection

The declaration that "now is Christ risen from the dead, and become the first fruits of them that slept" (1 Corinthians 15:20) assures us that there will be much fruit to follow, for "first fruits," in the Old Testament, was an offering of the earliest part of the harvest unto the Lord. After this offering was made, the harvest season began. The resurrection of the righteous dead is not only widely taught in the Bible, it is almost universally believed by Christians throughout the world. It is a fountainhead of our hope, for Paul admitted, "If in this life only we have hope in Christ, we are of all men most miserable" (1 Corinthians 15:19).

So closely does Paul parallel the resurrection of the saints with the resurrection of Christ that he wrote, "For if the dead rise not, then is not Christ raised: And if Christ be not raised, your faith is vain; ye are yet in your sins. Then they also which are fallen asleep in Christ are perished" (1 Corinthians 15:16–18). Paul could not see an either/or possibility; to him it was a both/and relationship. Christ rose; we shall rise! If either side of the equation is false, both sides are false. We shall rise because He rose; we shall rise as He rose; and we shall rise in the same power that caused our Lord to arise. The resurrections are parallel.

But while all of this is accurate and absolutely true—we shall enjoy a resurrection of our bodies—it cannot be what Paul is addressing when he declares that God "hath raised us up together . . . in Christ Jesus" (Ephesians 2:6). Here, again, we encounter that word *together,* and Paul continues to use the Greek suffix *sun,* this time appending it to *egeirō,* giving us *sunegeirō,* or "raised together." When the Old Testament was translated into Greek, giving us the Septuagint Version, the translators used this Greek word *egeirō* for the opening statement of Psalm 68, "Let God arise. . . ." As I establish in my book *Let God Arise,* it pictures God arising to get actively involved in the lives of the Israelites from the moment they left Sinai until they were securely settled in the land. A very literal meaning of this word is "to stand upright."

We have been conditioned to think of our resurrection as totally in the future, but in the sense of our spiritual resurrection Paul asserts that it is in the past: "hath raised us up together." At whatever point Christ was raised to stand upright and get involved with life again, we, too, were raised from spiritual death to spiritual life. So radical and drastic is this change that Paul wrote, "Therefore if any man be in Christ, he is a new creature; old things are passed away; behold, all things are become new" (2 Corinthians 5:17), and

Montgomery translates that last phrase as ". . . the old life has passed away; behold, the new life has come."

Our Ephesians passage is vitally concerned with this present resurrection that brings us into a whole new life. Paul asserts, "And you hath he quickened, who were dead in trespasses and sins. . . . But God . . . even when we were dead in sins, hath quickened us together with Christ . . . and hath raised us up together . . . in Christ Jesus" (Ephesians 2:1,4,5,6). We have been "quickened" in the here and now, and we have been "raised" in the nasty here and now. It is only our bodies that must await the sweet by-and-by before they can experience resurrection. Death, obviously, must precede resurrection.

So unremitting was Paul's concept of the parallel between Christ's resurrection and his new way of living that he affirmed, "I am crucified with Christ: nevertheless I live; yet not I, but Christ liveth in me: and the life which I now live in the flesh I live by the faith of the Son of God, who loved me, and gave himself for me" (Galatians 2:20). The Holy Spirit revealed to Paul that the only answer to a sinful nature was identification with the crucifixion of Jesus Christ. We must die with and in Him, for reformation and renovation are insufficient in dealing with the sinful nature; it must die! But this is only one-third of the story, for the Gospel is not merely the death of Jesus, but His subsequent resurrection and ascension. Therefore we are declared to have died with Christ, to have been quickened with Christ, and to have been raised with Him to be seated with Him in heavenly places. We are now spiritual partakers of the entire work of the Gospel. While there is a finality yet to be received, even the fractional part that we have as a living reality is more than sufficient to enable us to live victoriously and vitally in

this present life, for we are declared to be "more than con-
querors through him that loved us" (Romans 8:37).

The Performance of Christ's Resurrection

Although, admittedly, there were no eyewitnesses to
Christ's resurrection, we do have the record of the four Gospels of how the resurrection was discovered, and these ac-
counts, pieced together, seem to tell the story effectively.
The order seems to be that a life-giving energy from God the
Father pierced through the solid stone walls of the sepulchre
where Christ was laid and brought new life to the body that
had poured out its blood on Golgotha's soil. In this new life
Christ came through the grave clothes without disturbing
them, and as the angels rolled away the huge stone that had
formed the door to the tomb, Christ stepped out to allow
others to step in and to discover that He was not there. This
living Christ then appeared to the two Marys, to the two
disciples walking despondently to Emmaus, to Peter, to the
ten disciples in the Upper Room, to Thomas with these ten
disciples on another occasion and to many, many others.
One of the most important aspects of Christ's resurrection
was His return to live among the very people with whom He
had lived before His death on the cross. The resurrection returned Christ to His disciples and loved ones before it returned Him, permanently, to His Father.

Is not our participation in Christ's resurrection ordered
along similar lines? Our pardon for all our sins relieved us of
a great load of guilt, but it left us impotent and imprisoned
in our own form of sepulchre. It wasn't until the life of the
Spirit began to course through our beings, quickening us
and making us truly "living souls," that we began to deal

with the grave clothes that bound us in our tombs. Some of us were shrouded in religious activities, regulations, observances, and ritual, and we found them to be encumbering to the new life that had been received from the Spirit of God. Until we were able to work our way through them, we were very much alive but as immobile as an Egyptian mummy. Others were muffled and concealed behind yards of winding cloths of guilt, introspection, self-deprecation, fear of unacceptance, and self-pity. They had to learn that the quickening life of God enables them to step through these restrictions without even having to unwind them. God's method of release is not lengthy therapy; God prefers to merely impart life that enables us to rise above problems rather than to try to unravel each one through self-scrutiny. If we will move in the life of the Spirit, we can rise above the memories of past experiences and the wounds and limitations of past involvements with life and people. We may be unable to unwrap ourselves, but we can step through and leave the wrappings behind.

God does not give us life and then leave us in the place of death. Once we've learned to rise in newness of life in Christ Jesus, we can expect God to send His angels to open a way of escape. God not only remits the curse of sin, He also removes sin's power to captivate. This is the theme of the sixth chapter of Romans. "Now if we be dead with Christ," it tells us, "we believe that we shall also live with him; knowing that Christ being raised from the dead dieth no more; death hath no more dominion over him. . . . Likewise reckon ye also yourselves to be dead indeed unto sin, but alive unto God through Jesus Christ our Lord. Let not sin therefore reign in your mortal body, that ye should obey it in the lusts thereof.... For sin shall not have dominion over you.... Being then made free from sin, ye became the servants of righteousness" (Romans 6:8,9,11,14,18).

We who once were the victims of sin have now become victors over sin through the impartation of resurrection life into our experience. The door to our tomb has been opened forever, and if we ever enter it again, it will be out of a volitional desire to return to the place from which we were delivered, since an open door allows entrance as well as escape.

It is at this stage of our new experience in God that our friends and acquaintances discover that we are no longer among the dead. They search the old graveyard in vain for our company. When we finally meet them, they cannot help recognizing that something majestic and supernatural has happened to us. While there is much about us that is recognizable, conversely there is much about us that is entirely different. They see that we are living, but they cannot understand the nature of that life. Our resurrection will be discovered, but it will not necessarily be comprehended, for it is unearthly—it is spiritual—and the carnal mind cannot fathom the existence of such life, much less be capable of analyzing it.

The newborn baby doesn't have a clue as to what has just happened to it; it merely lives the life that was imparted until, through the process of maturity, understanding comes. Even so, the "raised ones" of Christ's children need not spend time trying to determine what they have received; they are too busy living as freed individuals who have been brought into a new life in God's kingdom. Fortunately, we do not have to comprehend and understand this life to live it—we merely need to receive it.

The resurrected Christ walked, talked, fellowshipped, ate, and ministered to His associates in His resurrection life, and so should we! The workings of sin alienated man from God, from himself, and from other people, but the workings of resurrection life restore fellowship and relationship in each area. Because of this life that the Gospel brings, we enjoy an intimacy with other believers that was impossible before the new life came. Paul told the Philippians, "I thank my God. . . . for your fellowship in the gospel from the first day until now; being confident of this very thing, that he which hath begun a good work in you will perform it until the day of Jesus Christ" (Philippians 1:3,4–6). There seems to be an automatic fellowship (the Greek word is *koinonia*) among those who have become participants in Christ's resurrection. There is an awareness of a commonality of family life that gives us a firm foundation for fellowship.

Furthermore, Paul affirms that God is working in us, so that what He began in our tomb will be perpetuated until the coming of Christ to usher us into the heavenly realms in spirit, soul, and body. Not only will the life be perpetuated, but what this life is doing in and through us will continue to be made manifest. This resurrection life is the life of God Himself, and He is working in us. What a basis this should be for confidence in ourselves.

If God is working in *me,* then I should be able to accept and love myself. I am not what I was, but by His action within me I am becoming what I shall be throughout all eternity. I need not fear reverting to my "old ways," for God is working in me. I don't have to live under the shadow of old limitations, for God's resurrection life is working in me now.

This realization also becomes a blessed basis for devel-

oping confidence in one another, for not only is God working in me, but He is equally working in *other believers* at the
same time. They, too, are being changed. Their limitations
are being replaced with God's unlimited abilities, and their
fears, failures, insecurities, and frustrations are being replaced with God's peace, ability, confidence, and hope.
They are actuated and motivated by the same divine life
that lives in me, so I can have confidence in them and relate
to them in honesty and trust.

Of course this would be just as true concerning the Body
of Christ in general. We are formed of very different races,
cultures, languages, and even religious persuasions, but we
are animated by a common life that continues to work in us.
It is never a common doctrine or a common experience that
forms the basis of confidence in the universal Church of
God. As a matter of fact, these have often become the basis
for division among us rather than being unifying factors.
But once we see the common resurrection life in all believers
and realize that God is working in all of us together, we find
a restored confidence in this Church, which is Christ's Body
on earth.

The Particularity of Christ's Resurrection

God "hath raised us up together . . ." (Ephesians 2:6). A
more radical contrast could hardly be found in human experience: raised up together from death to life; from darkness
to light; and from the kingdom of satan to the kingdom of
God's dear Son. Jesus as Christ came from hades to heaven;
we are raised from sin to salvation, from slavery to freedom,
and from the earthlies to the heavenlies. We are no longer
earthbound; we have received eternal life and we will never
be the same again.

This new life we have received as a replacement for our sin-cursed, death-condemned life affects our entire being. Our walk through this world is changed, for now we walk in the Spirit as a preventive to fulfilling the lusts of the flesh (*see* Galatians 5:16). Instead of living by our animal impulses or our intellectual reasonings, we have the inner guidance of the Holy Spirit, who has raised us to a newness of life in Christ Jesus. It is a totally different way of living, for the domination of humanism is replaced with the dominion of the Holy Spirit. We no longer follow the ways of the world; we follow the direction of God as revealed in His Word and as impressed upon us by His Spirit. Because of this we are spared many failures and can successfully sidestep many pitfalls. Our homes become "heavenly places" rather than "the gates of hell." Our relationship with others is founded on love rather than lust, and even the way we handle our money comes under the guidance of the Holy Spirit.

When resurrection life comes to the believer, it begins to affect his speech, not only in replacing cursing with blessing, but in causing the indwelt person to "speak the truth in love" (Ephesians 4:15). It is not merely that the person is more accurate in his statements, but that his words now reflect the gentle, loving nature of Christ, who declared that He was the truth. Since this resurrection life is the same life that functioned in Christ Jesus, it is expected that it would be communicated with the same graciousness and love that Jesus used, for the Scriptures speak of Christ's words being "gracious words" (Luke 4:22).

Of course, before any person's speech patterns can drastically change, there must be a change in the thought patterns. This is an expected end result of living in resurrection life, for we are told that our thought patterns should be on positive, wholesome, pure, and praiseworthy things, not on the negative and depraved things about which the nonresurrected person thinks (*see* Philippians 4:8).

Furthermore, we are told, "If ye then be risen with Christ, seek those things which are above, where Christ sitteth on the right hand of God. Set your affection on things above, not on things on the earth. For ye are dead, and your life is hid with Christ in God" (Colossians 3:1–3). So this resurrection life affects the way a person lives, the way he talks, the way he thinks, and even the object of his affection. This life makes him different from those who do not possess it. It is almost the difference between a stuffed animal in a museum and a live animal in a zoo. Outwardly they look very much alike, but inwardly one has a life-giving principle at work, while the other only gives the outer appearance of being alive.

Resurrection life does, indeed, effect a radical change in our state, but this change does not come through constant striving or disciplined control. This life makes us different—we're "new creatures. The old life has passed away; behold the new is come" (2 Corinthians 5:17 MONTGOMERY). We've put off the old man and put on the new; we've enjoyed a spiritual resurrection. We are in the world, but not of it (*see* John 17:11,14).

When Christ came forth from the tomb in resurrection life He was indisputably immortal, but He was in loving contact with mortals. He was eternal, but He continued to involve Himself in our time dimension. Before His death He consistently involved Himself with persons. He was not concerned with institutions and ceremonial law; He was interested in men and women! He regularly ministered life to them. After the resurrection Jesus continued to exhibit a concern for people and their needs. He seemed to visualize the true Church as being people rather than places, and He came to build that Church, so He poured Himself into people before and after His resurrection.

So should we, for we are built to minister the life of Jesus Christ to this world. We are instrumented to follow the direction of the Holy Spirit quite intuitively, for He has become our inner life, the animating principle of our being. Following His direction is little more than obeying the instincts of our spiritual life. If we follow these inner directions, we, like Christ, will reach out to people in the world who are hurting. We will share the love that has permeated our beings and offer the wisdom and counsel of the Holy Spirit to those who have lost their way.

The Purpose of Christ's Resurrection

If God's ultimate purpose is to get everything united together in Christ Jesus, and if this Jesus is the great mystery with which the world of mankind must reckon, then it is imperative that Jesus continue to function in the affairs of men until God's perfect will has been accomplished. If the method God chose was to prepare a body for His Son, then that body must be either indestructible or replaceable. In the scheme of things, one body would not be sufficient for Christ, so God prepared three bodies for Him. At Bethlehem God provided Christ a body that could die, thereby offering men salvation. At the resurrection God provided Christ a body that could live eternally and be seated in the heavenlies to function as our great High Priest. But by sharing this resurrection life with those who had accepted the atoning work of the cross, God provided a third body for

Christ: a body that could function on this earth. This Body is called "the Church," and it is Christ's representative here in this world.

Of course the Church is not an institution, code of ethics, or religious laws intended to govern lives; the Church is people filled with the resurrection life of the Holy Spirit living out Christ in the world. Viewed as a collective unit, the Church is a kingdom, not a subculture. It is united by a common life as well as a common king. Since the Church is not of this world, nothing the world can do will help or hinder it. Political powers have tried to help the Church, and other political forces have sought to destroy it, but the Church of the living God is unaffected by the actions of puny men. This living Church is indestructible, for its life is "hid with Christ in God" (Colossians 3:3).

Resurrection life enables us to accomplish God's intention for and through our life here in this world. We are His ambassadors (*see* 2 Corinthians 5:20) living in a heavenly embassy here on the earth, and as such we are representatives of heaven among men. Hence the reason for making us participants in resurrection life here on this earth is to *be* Christ in the world. We live by His life, and as we allow that life to be lived out through us we become the only visualization of Christ that the world will ever see. This is a great responsibility, but we have both the life and the authority for this, for we have been quickened, raised, and seated with Christ. From the position of Christ's throne we can faithfully represent Him here on the earth.

6

Seated Together With Christ

The first six verses of Ephesians 2 give us an interesting pair of triads that sit in contrasting juxtaposition. The first three verses declare that by nature we are: (1) dead in sins, (2) confined in the world system, and (3) controlled by our lusts; while verses five and six teach that by association we are: (1) quickened with Christ, (2) raised with Christ, and (3) seated with Christ. Because of God's love and mercy we are lifted from sin to salvation, from restriction to resurrection, and from sensual control to being seated in Christ.

Somewhat like Peter and John on the Mount of Transfiguration, or like John on the isle of Patmos, the people of God have been set in places where the privileges of heaven are enjoyed, where the atmosphere of heaven fills our spiritual nostrils, where the fellowship and the enjoyment of heaven are known, and where an elevation of spirit is experienced as if heaven were already begun. We are spiritually seated "together in heavenly places in Christ Jesus" (Ephesians 2:6).

Our Posture—"Made Us Sit..."

One of the characteristics of the life that is lived "according to the course of this world" (Ephesians 2:2) is restlessness. As a matter of fact, one of the Hebrew words we often translate as "wicked" or "wickedness" is *raw-shaw* which Robert Baker Girdlestone, in his book *Synonyms of the Old Testament,* says "is supposed originally to refer to the *activity,* the *tossing,* and the *confusion* in which the wicked live, and the perpetual agitation which they cause to others." Not only does the wicked person live in inward restlessness, but he creates a confusion and an agitation in those around him. Isaiah was very aware of this, for he wrote, "The wicked are like the troubled sea, when it cannot rest, whose waters cast up mire and dirt. There is no peace, saith my God, to the wicked" (Isaiah 57:20,21).

Sin destroys peace and tranquility, and the guilt that sin produces further disrupts any inner harmony that may have survived. The turmoil that churns in the inner being of persons without God is so great that most of them fear being alone with their thoughts, and quietness is such a punishment that they surround themselves with sound at all times.

Such was our condition until the love and grace of God rescued us from "the spirit that now worketh in the children of disobedience" (Ephesians 2:2). When the Spirit of Life came to our hearts, He brought with Him "love, joy, peace, longsuffering, gentleness, goodness, faith, meekness, temperance" (Galatians 5:22,23), which totally revised our inner disposition toward life. With our damning sins remitted, our dead spirits resurrected, and our depressed souls raised, our delivered selves are invited to be seated together in heavenly places in Christ Jesus. The struggle is over, the work is done, and we can now come into Christ's rest.

Hebrews 4 speaks at length about a rest being left to the people of God and twice urges us to enter into that rest. If this rest were all future, we would not be admonished to "labour therefore to enter into that rest" (Hebrews 4:11), but the rest is for us in the here and now. David's beautiful shepherd psalm assures us that "He maketh me to lie down in green pastures" (Psalms 23:2). Release from tension rather than generation of tension is God's goal for His saints.

Furthermore, if we are made to "sit together in heavenly places in Christ Jesus" (Ephesians 2:6), then we are in a beautiful place of safety, for earlier Paul had said of Christ Jesus, God ". . . set him at his own right hand in the heavenly places, Far above all principality, and power, and might, and dominion, and every name that is named, not only in this world, but also in that which is to come" (Ephesians 1:20,21). There could be no greater defensive position than to be seated in the heavenlies in Christ Jesus, for nothing can touch us until it touches Him, and He has been exalted far above everything. The Christian who has learned to be seated in Christ does not have much worry about the demons, for they are "under his feet" (Ephesians 1:22).

In the letter to the Hebrews we are twice told that Jesus "sat down," and each time it is as evidence that His work was finished. In the beginning of the letter it says that Christ, "Who being the brightness of his glory, and the express image of his person, and upholding all things by the word of his power, when he had by himself purged our sins, *sat down on the right hand of the Majesty on high*" (Hebrews 1:3, italics added). Later, when Christ is contrasted with the Old Testament priesthood, we read, "And every priest standeth daily ministering and offering oftentimes the same sacrifices, which can never take away sins: But this man, after he had offered one sacrifice for sins for ever, *sat down on the right hand of God*" (Hebrews 10:11,12, italics added).

The uses of the term *sat down* describe the finished redemptive work of Christ—everything that needed to be done was completed—so Christ sat down in a position of rest and authority with God the Father. When we read in Ephesians that God has "made us sit together in heavenly places in Christ Jesus" (Ephesians 2:6), this cannot help suggesting the completed work of Christ in the initial salvation of the believer and the subsequent union with Himself that this redemptive work produces.

We are not to work at union with Christ; we are just to accept it as a finished work and sit at rest with Him in heaven. If man's efforts could have redeemed him, Christ would not have come, but He did come, and His redemptive work is absolute. Our faith in His provision enables us to sit with Him rather than strive with or for Him. We are made to sit, not to struggle!

Our Partner—"In Christ Jesus"

The New English Bible translates this verse "And in union with Christ Jesus he raised us up and enthroned us with him in the heavenly realms" (Ephesians 2:6 NEB). All of the action—quickened, raised, seated—is by virtue of our union with Christ Jesus. Apart from Him we are still dead in our trespasses and sins, but united in Him we have been both made alive and placed in heavenly places. This is never a unilateral action; it is always a united achievement. God has so placed us "in" Christ that whatever He does for Jesus automatically accrues to our benefit.

In making us children of God He inseparably linked us with His only begotten Son, Jesus Christ. The Roman letter says, "The Spirit itself beareth witness with our spirit that we are the children of God. And if children, then heirs; heirs of God, and joint-heirs with Christ; if so be that we suffer with him, that we may be also glorified together" (Romans

8:16,17). It is mind boggling enough to conceive of ourselves as "heirs of God," but it is almost beyond our level of faith to accept that we are actually "joint-heirs with Christ." That God has chosen to share some of His riches with us is one thing, but that He has given us equal access to everything that is His along with Jesus Christ is quite another; but that is exactly what "joint-heirs" means. An attorney once explained to me that "joint-heirship" means that each owns all, and illustrated it by referring to a joint checking account. Each partner to this checking account has access to everything that is in the account; it is not a fifty-fifty division. Everything that God has made available to His Son, Christ Jesus, is also and equally available to us.

Since we are joint-heirs with Christ "that we may be also glorified together" (Romans 8:17), it is to be expected, then, that when Christ was lifted into the heavenlies and seated at the right hand of the Father we, too, would be raised with Him and seated in Him on the throne. We are partners together in everything that God does for Christ Jesus. The authorities that God has granted to Him, He in turn has granted to the Church. The position to which God exalted Him, He has chosen to share with the members of His earthly body, and the power that God invested in Christ, He in turn invested in the Church. We are not merely joint-heirs on paper; we are partners with Christ Jesus in fact.

Although a joint-heirship could exist between persons who were hostile one to the other, the joint beneficiary partnership between the saints on earth and Christ in heaven is based upon a close association one with the other. Jesus told His disciples, "Apart from me you can do nothing" (John 15:5 RSV), and it is equally true that apart from Christ we *have* nothing. Just as the priests of the Old Testament were not granted an inheritance with their brethren, so that God could be their entire inheritance, so it is our relationship to Jesus, not to fellow believers, that insures our participation in the heavenly inheritance. Paul declared, "... For all things are yours; ... And ye are Christ's; and Christ is God's" (1 Corinthians 3:21,23). The link is from God, to Christ, to us.

Our Place—"In Heavenly Places"

If we are to be seated "in Christ," it must be where He is, and He is not on this earth (except as represented by His Spirit). He is in the heavens, seated at the Father's right hand. Since the word *places* (Ephesians 2:6) is in italics in our King James Version, where italics are used to indicate that the word has been supplied by the translators, some have preferred to merely speak of our being "in Christ in the heavenlies." But that is a bit too ambiguous for most modern translators. Phillips translates it as "in Christ Jesus in the Heavens," while the Jerusalem Bible says, "and gave us a place with him in heaven." The New English Bible, the Living Bible, and the New International Version all use the phrase "in the heavenly realms," while Today's English Version merely calls it "the heavenly world."

No matter what translation you may choose, it seems obvious that this is more than an emotional experience that becomes "heavenly." It is speaking of a literal place—a place Jesus called "heaven." We who are earthbound because of our physical bodies are declared to have a position in Christ Jesus that is in heaven. To our present spiritual revelation there is nothing higher than this in all of God's creation, and yet we are declared to be there.

The position heaven holds is illustrated in Paul's discussion about the power of God "which he exerted in Christ when he raised him from the dead, when he enthroned him at his right hand in the heavenly realms, far above all government and authority, all power and dominion, and any title of sovereignty that can be named, not only in this age but in the age to come. He put everything in subjection beneath his feet, and appointed him as supreme head to the church, which is his body and as such holds within it the fullness of him who himself receives the entire fullness of God" (Ephesians 1:20–22 NEB). Unconditional authority, unlimited power, and ultimate position have been granted to Christ, and we are "joint-heirs" with Him in it. He, and we, look down from the top, and we are untouchable by things in the human and satanic realms. None can exert an authority over us, for we are already positioned in the One who has the highest authority in all of creation. Everything has been put under Christ's feet, and since we are partners with Him and are seated in Him on the throne of heaven, everything, then, is also put under our feet.

Most of the battles Christians fight are because they fail to understand their lofty position in Christ. They are threatened by something that has no actual authority over them, and they worry about things that cannot happen to them as long as they are in Christ Jesus.

A pastor met a parishioner of his in a grocery store and asked him, "How are you, John?"

"Oh, pastor," he replied, "I'm pretty good, under the circumstances."

"But, John," the pastor responded, "what are you doing

under the circumstances when you are seated in Christ Jesus in heaven?"

How can we be under anything when we are over everything in Christ Jesus our Lord?

"Seated with Christ in heaven" is superior even to Adam's relationship, for Adam had to await God's arrival in the garden of Eden before he could have fellowship with Him. As glorious as that fellowship was, it was limited to God's appearances. Furthermore, that fellowship was broken by sin and Adam was driven out of the garden forever, deprived of his authorities, and cursed by the very things he once controlled.

At Bethlehem God's love came down to man and met him at his low level. It was a condescending love. But at Calvary God's love lifted man to God's level—it was an ascending love that lifted man from the lowest to the highest, or as preachers enjoy putting it, "from the guttermost to the uttermost." We who once were "alienated from the life of God" (Ephesians 4:18) are now aligned with that life and allowed to sit in Christ, the source of all divine life, in the heavens.

Our Position—Reigning Regents

That Jesus Christ is now "KING OF KINGS, AND LORD OF LORDS" (Revelation 19:16) is not only declared in the heavens, but it is recognized in His Church and will soon be enforced in the world. When Jesus was born He was searched for as "King of the Jews" (Matthew 2:2). As He entered into public ministry His main theme was "the kingdom of God is at hand" (Mark 1:15), and at His death "Pilate wrote an inscription to be fastened to the cross; it read, 'Jesus of Nazareth King of the Jews' " (John 19:19 NEB). He

was born, He lived, and He died as a King. When God
raised Christ from the dead, the eternal reign of our Lord
and Christ continued as though it had never been interrupted by murderous men. He was, and is, and ever shall be
"KING OF KINGS."

If we are seated *in* Christ Jesus *in* the heavens, then we are
not only *where* He is but we become part of *what* He is. If He
is a King, and we are partakers of His nature and His exal-
tation, then we share in His kingly role as vice-kings. This
seems to be the emphasis of Peter when he declares that we
are a "royal priesthood" (1 Peter 2:9) and the message of
John when he writes that God "hath made us kings and
priests unto God and his Father"; or "hast made us unto our
God kings and priests: and we shall reign on the earth"
(Revelation 1:6; 5:10). While it is true that some of the modern translators have preferred to translate this "a kingdom
of priests," it is equally true that many translators have held
to the form our King James Version uses. The promise that
"we shall reign on the earth" (Revelation 5:10) fits the concept of a king rather than a priest, although there was a period in Israel's history when priests ruled the people.

While some teachers have enjoyed putting all of this into
some future pigeonhole, the Bible speaks of the appoint-
ment as past and the action as in the present. "Hath made
us ..." "Ye *are* ... a royal priesthood." While it is very
likely that there is a future fulfillment involved here, we
cannot escape the present reality of being kings in our present life, reigning cooperatively with Christ Jesus; for reigning in life is one of Paul's consistent themes in his Epistles.

We are not reigning *for* Christ; we are reigning *with*
Christ. It is not so much delegated authority as it is shared
authority. For instance, I can sign a power of attorney and

delegate authority to someone to do a specific business transaction in my name, but since my wife and I consistently enter into all business transactions as co-owners, there is no need to delegate authority; we merely share authority. Since each owns all, each has authority over what is owned. In allowing us to be "joint-heirs" with Christ, God also granted us areas of authority or kingliness, and these areas are discussed and illustrated in the Scriptures.

The most obvious area of rule that Christ shares with us is our personal life. Redemption does not remove our volitional freedom; it restores it. Sin and satan had taken away our right of choice, but God rehabilitated it when He quickened and raised us up with Christ Jesus. God has not chosen to dominate His saints like a benevolent dictator; rather, He has chosen to vest authority for the personal life in each of us. We are not without divine counsel, enablement, and guidelines, but each person is expected to reign in Christ over his own life. The wise man said, "He that is slow to anger is better than the mighty; and he that ruleth his spirit than he that taketh a city" (Proverbs 16:32). Until we have learned to rule our own spirit we certainly are unfit to rule another's spirit. One of the outstanding characteristics of the man of the world is the frequency with which he is out of control. His temper rules him, his passions control him, his bodily appetites dominate him, and his emotions direct his life. The unconverted are dominated by their bodies and souls, but the children of God are challenged to rule their lives from their spirits, for that portion of their lives is in fellowship and in authority with God.

A second obvious area where the believer is challenged to be a regent with Christ Jesus is the home. What a shambles sin is making of the homes in America. The divorce rate climbs higher and higher year after year, and tension, abuse, adultery, and neglect run rampant in many of the marriages that stay together. Even Christian marriages suffer repeated attacks against them. It is time that we learn to exercise our God-given authority to our homes. Husbands need to discipline themselves to consistently love their wives (*see* Ephesians 5:25,28,33); wives need to "submit yourselves unto your own husbands, as unto the Lord" (Ephesians 5:22), which, by the way, is not difficult when the husband is loving the wife "even as Christ also loved the church, and gave himself for it" (Ephesians 5:25); and both parents need to "train up a child in the way he should go: and when he is old, he will not depart from it" (Proverbs 22:6) rather than to abdicate the rulership of the home to the children. These areas of rulership are so important that in listing the qualifications for individuals who will rule in the Church, Paul disqualifies anyone who lacks self-discipline or who does not have control of his own home. As surely as "charity begins at home," rulership also begins in the smaller segment of society.

If our Christian society were no larger than our homes, our authority might well stop there; but God blends families together into active components of His Church on earth, and they need a "king" over them, so God has appointed officers in this Church to function as regents with Christ Jesus. Paul declared that following the ascension of Christ "he . . . gave some to be apostles, some to be prophets, some to be evangelists, and some to be pastors and teachers, to prepare God's people for works of service, so that the body of Christ may be built up until we all reach unity in the faith . . . and become mature, attaining to the whole measure of the fullness of Christ" (Ephesians 4:11–13 NIV). These gifted persons became gifts to the Church. As someone has pointed out, the apostle governs, the prophet guides, the evangelist gathers, the pastor guards, and the teacher grounds. These offer spiritual guidance, authority, and direction while the members of the Body of Christ are growing into maturity. They do not set up personal kingdoms; they reign as governors with Christ in the kingdom of God, which is seen on the earth in the Church.

Furthermore, there are administrative helps God has placed in the Church on earth to help in its government. We read of elders, deacons, musicians, givers, administrators, and so forth. The area of rule may be more limited, but God shares authority in proportion to our ability to function in that authority. Whether it is only in our personal lives or in the Church itself, God has chosen us to be vice-rulers with Christ Jesus.

Positional or Conditional?

"Made us to sit together in heavenly places in Christ Jesus" (Ephesians 2:6) seems almost too good to be true. Are we actually in a place of rest, safety, satisfaction, partnership, and authority with Christ, or are we still restlessly here on the earth insecure, unsatisfied, often alone, and classified as a member of a minority group?

Some teachers who have caught sight of being seated in Christ in the heavens can speak of the truth so positively that we almost expect to leave our bodies and ascend to heaven right there and then, while other teachers so greatly emphasize our conflict with sin, satan, and self in the nasty here and now that we can't even imagine what heaven could be like.

Who is correct? Both are! Positionally we have been

placed in Christ in heaven, but conditionally we are still here on the earth in human bodies, contending with ungodliness on every side. It is the difference between our standing and our state. Because of the love and mercy of God He has declared that our standing is in heaven with Christ Jesus. This is His provision, and He sees it as performed. Still, we have not yet been fully redeemed, for we await the redemption of our bodies. Our state is earthly while our standing is heavenly. Our position is in Christ, while our condition is in the world. We have been "made the righteousness of God in him [Christ]" (2 Corinthians 5:21), although we continue to struggle with many unrighteous thoughts, desires, ambitions, and actions. We are "complete in him" (Colossians 2:10), but we live in a sense of great imperfection.

Some years ago when I was in prayer the Lord told me that it was about time for me to see myself as He saw me. For quite a lengthy time He described ministries into which I had not yet come, graces that I knew I did not possess, and positions I never aspired to attain. When I remonstrated with Him saying that He certainly could not be describing me, He told me that He was describing me from the blueprints, and Master Builder that He was, He could see the completed structure in the plans. In contrast to this, I was viewing myself by my present stage of construction—a gouged hole in the ground with some footing poured and reinforcing rods rusting as they stuck up in the air unsupported. The difference was that He could see me as I was becoming in Christ, while I viewed myself as I was right then in life.

What God has purposed, He is competently able to perform, so He can declare us to be in Christ while we are actually still in the world. He can declare us to be righteous while much unrighteousness continues to be worked out of our natures. He can position us as kings with Christ Jesus even though we desperately need another to rule over our lives, for God sees the end from the beginning.

We are not yet totally spiritual beings; we live in earthly tabernacles and are subject to the pressures of life. But we are at least one-third spiritual beings, and that part of us reigns with Christ Jesus in the heavens.

The Purpose Is Togetherness With Christ

We dare not lose sight of the fact that it is Christ's life, resurrection, ascension, and throne that are in view here in Ephesians. In the declaration that we, too, have been quickened, raised, and seated, it is always "together with Christ." Very much as the wife shares the honor and possessions of her husband because of her relationship to him, so we share Christ's conquests, glory, and positions because of our intimate relationship with Him. We cannot be participants in them without Him, but what we cannot do He has already done for us, and He has offered to share this with His saints.

We've seen that the ultimate *purpose* of togetherness is to bring all things in heaven and on earth together under Christ. The *process* is to bring the saints into this relationship right now by quickening them together with Christ, raising them up with Christ, and causing them to sit together with Christ Jesus in the heavenlies.

But this is not the end; it is the process. What does God intend to produce by this process? What is the *product* God has in mind in getting us together with Christ as individuals?

Section III

God's Product of
Getting Us Together

Now therefore ye are no more strangers and foreigners, but fellowcitizens with the saints, and of the household of God; And are built upon the foundation of the apostles and prophets, Jesus Christ himself being the chief corner stone; In whom all the building fitly framed together groweth unto an holy temple in the Lord: In whom ye also are builded together for an habitation of God through the Spirit.

Ephesians 2:19–22

7

We Are Framed Together

Getting us together with Christ is relatively easy compared with getting us together with one another. As long as we deal exclusively with the mystical, we have few miseries, but when the Spirit begins to deal with the practical outworkings of this mystical union with Christ Jesus, we face potential conflict and confusion, because being framed together is not something done entirely for us; it is done in and through us. Whenever God allows us to be a participant in His workings, it usually slows down the operation and introduces conflicting wills, but since God has eternity in which to accomplish His purposes, He can outwait our childlike reticence while slowly showing us that His plan excels ours.

This plan that He is unfolding to us reveals that God not only intends to get believers together with Christ Jesus in heavenly places, but He also intends to get these believers together during their sojourn here in earthly places. We are being united with fellow believers into a "holy temple in the Lord" (Ephesians 2:21) to ultimately become "an habitation of God through the Spirit" (Ephesians 2:22). We are now in Christ, but God wants to unite us in such a way that God can be in us here on the earth.

United Together As Citizens of a Country

Having declared in the second chapter of Ephesians that we have been quickened, raised, and seated together in heavenly places in Christ Jesus, and that we Gentiles who "... were without Christ, being aliens from the commonwealth of Israel, and strangers from the covenants of promise, having no hope, and without God in the world ... are made nigh by the blood of Christ" (Ephesians 2:12,13), the Holy Spirit tells us that we "are no longer foreigners and aliens, but fellow citizens with God's people ..." (Ephesians 2:19 NIV).

"Fellow citizens with the saints" is the way the King James expresses it. This is in contrast to the status of "foreigners" that we Gentiles formerly had. Paul is likely thinking of an ancient city-state, which was made up of free citizens and also of resident aliens who could exercise no civil rights. To this he adds the class who were not even residents but outsiders altogether—aliens. We had no part in the commonwealth of Israel, but now that God is building His Church of both Jews and Gentiles, the members of that Church all have the rank of free citizens. None of us has an inferior status, but each of us is in the fullest sense a fellow citizen with the saints. In this new country—or, to be more technically accurate, this new kingdom—we are a body of free citizens experiencing something similar to what Roman citizenship conferred upon individuals in the days of Paul. And how he rejoiced in the privileges, protection, and provisions that Roman citizenship afforded him.

Whatever privileges, protection, and provisions are available to one in God's kingdom are available to all of the saints, for we are fellow citizens of equal standing in our residency here on the earth. The religious institution has artificially established a caste system with a hierarchy and a "lower-archy" that will range from pope to parishioner in one system, and from clergy to laity in another; but God's true kingdom—God's invisible Church—offers an equality of citizenship. All are loyal to the same authority, obedient to the same laws, and inheritors of the same rights.

United Together As Members of a Family

The Jewish Christians claimed, by right of their descent, to be God's people *par excellence.* They felt that they were the select of God's elect, but the Holy Spirit not only says that we who have been united with Christ are fellow citizens in God's kingdom; He affirms that we are "members of God's household" (Ephesians 2:19 NIV). In *The Moffatt New Testament Commentary,* E. F. Scott says, "Or perhaps (as in 1:18) the word *saints* should be rendered 'the holy ones,' i.e. the heavenly company. Hitherto the Gentiles have been denied all privileges even on earth; now they have been admitted to equality with angels (cf. Heb. 12:23). This may be in Paul's mind when he says that they have become not merely fellow-citizens but members of *God's own household.* As the people of Christ they belong to the inner circle, like those servants of a king who form his immediate retinue."

Paul speaks of this great family of God in his prayer as he says, "For this cause I bow my knees unto the Father of our Lord Jesus Christ, of whom the whole family in heaven and earth is named" (Ephesians 3:14,15). What a heritage; what an honor; what fellowship is ours as members of God's family, some of whom are residents of heaven already, and others who are still inhabitants of the earth. Although there may not be equality of ability or responsibility in the members of this family, there is equality of relationship both with our common Father and with our brothers and sisters in Christ.

We who were "without Christ and aliens" have now become "members of God's household" (NIV); "members of the family of God" (TEV); "members of God's very own family, citizens of God's country, and you belong in God's household with every other Christian" (TLB), all because we have been quickened, raised, and seated together with Christ. We are united not merely by mutual interests or covenant arrangements but by the clinging instincts of family affection. We are not merely friends with fellow believers, for we can choose our friends. We are brothers and sisters in the faith, and no one can choose his kinfolk. We have to learn to accept them because they, like we, are born into the same family and have the same rights and privileges that we do.

So we have both an equality of citizenship in the kingdom and an equality of relationship in the family. God has no favorites, has not established a slave system, nor has He adopted any orphans. We are all "sons of God" and citizens of heaven's kingdom on earth.

United Together As Sections of a Building

In just a few verses Paul shifts the imagery from state, to sons, to stones, and our togetherness progresses from being fellow citizens of God's kingdom, to being filial family members of God's household, to being fitly framed together as portions of God's living temple. In some respects the parts of a building are more united than even the members of a family, for in a well-constructed edifice one part is so dependent upon another that to disturb a portion would be to injure the whole.

What may seem to be a rather abrupt transition from a commonwealth to a building would not seem incongruous to the residents of Ephesus. Fundamentally it is but a transition from a political and social to a material image, and to the Ephesians, whose temple to Diana was the pride and center of their political and social as well as religious life, the shifting would seem comfortable.

In ancient times a temple was not so much a place for worship, like a modern church, but was considered the actual dwelling place of their god. Their worship was conducted in the space outside the temple, while the temple itself was reserved for the deity and for the priests who supposedly ministered to that god's desires.

Divine revelation to Israel broke through this primitive conception and made God's people aware of a God "who dwelleth not in temples made with hands" (*see* Acts 7:48), and the life, the work, and the teaching of Jesus Christ caused the belief that God dwelt in a visible earthly house to give place to a higher view that God's true servants constituted His temple. Christianity immediately accepted this lofty creed, and in a variety of passages Paul declares that God has His abode in the Church—in a society of men and women who have entered into fellowship with Him. ". . . Ye are the temple of the living God," Paul wrote; "as God hath said, I will dwell in them, and walk in them; and I will be their God, and they shall be my people" (2 Corinthians 6:16).

The *Pulpit Commentary* says, "All whom Christ reconciles are parts of a grand temple. (a) Beautifully united: 'framed together.' (b) Gradually advancing: 'groweth.' (c) Religiously consecrated: 'a holy temple.' What a glorious temple this is! The temple of Diana these Ephesians originally considered as the glory of the world, but it would appear to them contemptible by the grand spiritual temple that Paul here pictures to their imagination."

This spiritual Temple is the first evident product of God's program of getting us together. The most normally used New Testament word for it is *Church,* although any student with a good concordance could probably find thirty or more collective nouns used to describe this same body of believers. In the connotation of a building the Church is called the House of Christ (Hebrews 3:6), the House of God (1 Timothy 3:15), the Habitation of God (Ephesians 2:19–22), the Temple of God (1 Corinthians 3:16,17), the Temple of the Living God (2 Corinthians 6:16), and God's Building (1 Corinthians 3:9).

In his book *All the Doctrines of the Bible,* Herbert Lockyer reminds us, "We must get it out of our minds that in the first century a *church* consisted of bricks and mortar. What the apostles meant by a church was not an edifice with pulpit, chancel and pews, but a congregation or society of regenerated people built together like living stones and content to meet in some upper room in private dwellings like that of Mary, mother of John Mark."

The true Church is people filled with the Holy Spirit, living out Christ in the world. Collected and fitted together, they form a dwelling place, or holy habitation, for God Himself, for God dwells in His Church on the earth. His communication is to that Church, and His acts are performed through that Church. The Father loved the Church, the Son died for the Church, and the Holy Spirit dwells in that Church.

The Architect of the Church

In the challenging roll call of faith, Abraham is credited with "looking forward to the city with firm foundations, whose architect and builder is God" (Hebrews 11:10 NEB). All the while Abraham and Sarah traversed the promised land, living in portable tents, they kept their eyes open for that permanent city that God Himself had designed and was constructing. With the aid of further New Testament revelation we know that it was not the Jerusalem of David's time that Abraham sought, but the New Jerusalem that shall come down out of heaven and be the abode of the saints of God (*see* Revelation 21). But when John saw this city coming down he spoke of it ". . . as a bride adorned for her husband. And I heard a great voice out of heaven saying, Behold, the tabernacle of God is with men, and he will dwell with them, and they shall be his people, and God himself shall be with them, and be their God" (Revelation 21:2,3). In preluding his description of the heavenly city with a presentation of the Bride (which is merely another term for the Church), John seems to incorporate the Church as an integral part of the New Jerusalem. Perhaps the Church is the earthly portion of the construction that shall yet be joined to the heavenly part.

This same concept seems to be presented in the next chapter of Hebrews: "Ye are come unto mount Sion, and unto the city of the living God, the heavenly Jerusalem . . ." (Hebrews 12:22). The action is in the present, "ye *are* come," so it must refer to the part of heaven that is now on earth—the

Church. God is the Architect of both the Church and the New Jerusalem.

The same Architect of the whole is the Architect of the part; God has blueprinted and is building His Church. That God's program, which includes the Church, had its origins on the drawing board in heaven long before our world was formed is taught repeatedly in the New Testament (*see* 2 Timothy 1:9; Titus 1:2; 1 Peter 1:2,20). Master Architect that He is, God predesigned the coming together of the reconciled ones to be formed into a dwelling place for God on the earth.

God designed that His people would *become* His temple, not that they would *build* Him a temple. When David offered to build God a house, God responded by sending Nathan the prophet with the message, "Shalt thou build me an house for me to dwell in? . . . the Lord telleth thee that he will make thee an house" (2 Samuel 7:5,11). David was unable to construct a place for God to dwell, but God offered to build a permanent household for the king. Men do not build God a place to inhabit; God builds His own dwelling place out of men united into a holy habitation.

As Herbert Lockyer reminds us, "Thus the Church is not of human creation, nor the outcome of any merely natural tendency on the part of men to form a society which will give expression and effect to their faith; it is of divine origin, being fashioned above.

"It is God's Church (Galatians 1:13), and as such it is doubly dependent on Him. It was originated by Him. It is a building which He has reared (1 Corinthians 3:9). It is also dependent upon Him for support."

When we look at other things that God has designed, observing the intricate details that He has built into the smallest items of our known world, and, conversely, when we view the unlimited magnitude of His design in the heavens above us, we gain a tremendous respect for the talent and ability of the great Architect of the Church. How marvelous it will be when the construction of His latest project, the Church, is completed. If He has saved the best for the last, it will be mind boggling.

The Foundation

Wise Master Builder that He is, God laid a solid, sure foundation for His Church, knowing full well that nothing that is built in the superstructure is of any value unless the foundation is sufficient. When Peter made his great confession of faith, Jesus responded by saying, ". . . upon this rock I will build my church; and the gates of hell shall not prevail against it" (Matthew 16:18). Surely Christ was not going to build His Church on Peter, but upon that which Peter had just seen by revelation—the reality that Jesus was indeed the Christ, the Son of God. This forms the fundamental foundation for the entire Church, and its steadfastness is so certain that nothing hell can do will prevail against that which is built upon it. The Church is builded upon the Rock Christ Jesus.

In his letter to the church at Corinth, Paul wrote, "For other foundation can no man lay than that is laid, which is Jesus Christ" (1 Corinthians 3:11), while in the Ephesian letter he declared that "you are built upon the foundation laid by the apostles and prophets, and Christ Jesus himself is the foundation-stone" (Ephesians 2:20 NEB). In his *Expositions of Holy Scripture,* Dr. Alexander Maclaren writes:

A question may here rise as to the meaning of "prophets." Unquestionably the expression in other places of the Epistle does mean New Testament prophets, but seeing that here Jesus is designated as the foundation stone which, standing beneath two walls, has a face into each, and binds them strongly together, it is more natural to see in the prophets the representatives of the great teachers of the old dispensation as the apostles were of the new. The remarkable order in which these two classes are named, the apostles being first, and the prophets who were first in time being last in order of mention, confirms this explanation, for the two co-operating classes are named in the order in which they lie in the foundation. Digging down you come to the more recent first, to the earlier second, and deep and massive, beneath all, to the corner-stone on whom all rests, in whom all are united together . . . Paul rejoices to discern the ancient stones firmly laid by long dead hands.

Other writers feel that the Old Testament prophets lacked any revelation of the Church and therefore could not have become the foundation for the Church. They argue that it was the New Testament prophets, of whom the apostles were notable, who formed the foundation of the Church. The names of the prophets on the foundation stones of the heavenly Jerusalem would argue for the Old Testament prophets, plus the declaration of the Bible that ". . . the testimony of Jesus is the spirit of prophecy" (Revelation 19:10). But the argument is unprofitable, for the nugget of truth that Paul is sharing is that the materials composing the foundation of the Church are *living* stones—teachers and proclaimers of the truth—but Christ, as the one foundation, is the "chief cornerstone." The foundation of the Church is not so much in the witnesses of the truth as in the truth itself. The apostles and prophets laid the first course in the foundation of the Church, and were careful to recognize and build only one foundation, united and held together by the one cornerstone—Christ Jesus. This Christ-centeredness of both the Old and New Testament writers assures us that the foundation is deep and broad, and can never be removed and replaced by any human structure. From the Old Testament through the New Testament God was laying a foundation for His Church, and nothing that this twentieth century can come up with will function as an adequate substitute.

The Cornerstone

That Jesus Christ is the cornerstone of this holy temple in the Lord is clearly stated, but just what is intended by this phrase is open for discussion. The fact that this cornerstone is spoken of in conjunction with the foundation would lead many to believe that it refers to the four main corners of the foundation, and with that in view the New English Bible calls it "the foundation-stone." If we would remind ourselves that the foundations in Paul's day were not poured concrete but hewn stone, we might better understand the metaphor. The first stone placed would become the bench mark from which all measurements for the foundation would be taken. In this sense, then, Jesus is clearly the "foundation-stone."

Most translations, however, prefer to use the term "cornerstone," which brings to our mind the decorative and engraved stone we place in a building after the building itself is complete. It honors the builder and often contains various memorabilia consistent with the nature of the use of the building. That this was also done in Paul's day is argued by some, and that Christ Jesus is God's depository of all things precious to heaven is indisputable. Furthermore, Christ is the honoree of this building, and certainly His name would be on such a stone. But this can hardly be what Paul was speaking of, for this "cornerstone" is mentioned right after the foundation is discussed, not at the time of the dedication of the building.

Laying stone has been a hobby of mine for many years, and I can testify that all masonry work, whether stone, brick, block, or tile, starts by building up the corners of the wall. These are often called the cornerstones, or corner blocks, or whatever. These corners are laid with great precision, for they will determine the dimensions of the building, the width of the joints to which the stones are laid, and will set the pattern in which the other stones are to be laid. A line is stretched between these corners and the stones or bricks are laid to this line. Is not Paul saying that Christ has become the corner of this great temple? God placed Him in precise position that He might establish the dimensions of the building, the pattern in which the stones are to be laid, and even predetermine the width of the mortar joints between the stones.

Most of the stonework we see here in America is mere facing, that is, it is a decorative exterior laid against a pre-built wall. But the building of which Paul is speaking is actually constructed of stones—they are the structural material that forms the building. By the very nature of this form of construction, work is usually begun on more than one wall simultaneously, with the masons building toward the same corner. Remembering that the context of chapter 2 of Ephesians concerns itself with the great differences between the Jews and the Gentiles, and that God was making of the two one "new man" (Ephesians 2:15), is it not possible that this "cornerstone" is the joining force between them?

In *Calvin's Commentaries,* John Calvin writes, "He means that Jews and Gentiles were two separate walls, but are formed into one spiritual building. Christ is placed in the middle of the corner for the purpose of uniting both, and this is the force of the metaphor." Alexander Maclaren sees it similarly, for he wrote, "The stone laid beneath the two walls which diverge at right angles from each other binds both together and gives strength and cohesion to the whole."

Remove the cornerstone and the two walls are subject to falling. Jesus is the stone that ties the different walls of the Church together, so that rather than weakening one another, each draws strength from the other because of their union in Christ, the cornerstone.

So whether we see this as the "foundation-stone," the commemorative stone, the built-up corner, or the stone that ties the two walls together, Jesus Christ is God's cornerstone in the Church here on the earth. By Him all things consist and hold together. We are built upon Him, built according to Him, and are built into Him.

Fitly Framed Together

Once more Paul uses the prefix *sun,* "with," and affixes it to two other Greek words—*harmos,* "a joint," and *legō,* "to choose"—giving us *sunarmologeō,* which is translated "fitly framed together" here in Ephesians 2:21. In his book *An Expository Dictionary of New Testament Words,* W. E. Vine agrees with this translation, adding, "[it] . . . is used metaphorically of the Church as a spiritual temple, the parts being 'fitly framed together.'"

In our Western culture, when we speak of a building being "framed" we refer to the rough structure that will form the shell of the incomplete building. It is the foundation, the subfloor, stud walls, and roof. Some carpenters specialize in framing, and leave all other work to tradesmen who complete the structure. Although in Paul's time most construction was masonry construction, the principle still obtains. The foundation, the cornerstones, and the archways that formed the doorways and window openings were laid first—they framed the building yet to come. The location, the dimensions, and the style of building were determined by this framing. We might say that this outlined the building, and others filled in that outline, or that the framing forms the skeleton that gives both form and structural strength to the finished building.

In a very real sense, God is framing His Church here and now. He has laid its foundation so the location and dimensions are already predetermined. The corners and all archways have been built up, and weight-bearing pilasters that will support the roof structure are in place. As both the Architect and the Builder, He is keeping Himself involved in all steps of the construction to be certain that the engineering is carried out in detail. God is building for eternity, and not merely for time, so the structure must be solid, strong, sturdy, and secure.

If you have ever seen a modern office building or a skyscraper under construction you will be able to visualize our imagery. After the foundation has been poured and set, the building rises on vertical columns of concrete intersected about every ten feet with a floor. It is nothing more than a skeleton; yet in that skeleton is all the structural engineering for the entire building. Other things will be added for utility, decoration, safety, and comfort, but the essential building is engineered around that skeletal structure.

So it is with God's Church. God first builds the framework and then completes the walls, plumbing, electrical work, and heating. Since Paul clearly defines the foundation and the chief cornerstone, and Peter defines the keystone or "headstone" (which would signify that the arches are already in place), we saints are more spectators of this framing than we are participants. In the sense that we are "in Christ" we have become part of this skeletal structure, but in God's wisdom and grace He has not made the Church dependent upon the strength of materials such as you and I. Far stronger materials than this have been used by the Master Builder as He constructs His Church. While we do, of course, have a part in the building, we will be used in areas where structural strength is not so critical.

In the *Moffatt New Testament Commentary,* Dr. E. F. Scott, of Union Theological Seminary, comments, "It is the power of Christ which orders the harmonious progress of the building, and the work is therefore described as being accomplished in him. He is not merely the foundation but, so to speak, the frame in which everything is contained."

Jesus Christ is undeniably God's structural framework for the Church. Everything rests on Him, is dependent upon Him, and fits firmly into Him. Without Him, there can be no Church. Wherever the work of Christ is refused or His ministry is resisted, that area of the Church becomes rubble. It doesn't matter how decorative the marble slabs on the office building may look; they are totally dependent upon the skeletal structure, and no matter how beautiful our individual ministries may become, they must always remain firmly attached to the finished work of Jesus Christ or they will fall to the ground, endangering all who happen to be standing beneath us. In speaking of Jesus, Paul wrote, "For in him dwelleth all the fulness of the Godhead bodily. And ye are complete in him, which is the head of all principality and power" (Colossians 2:9,10). It is not Christ who is completed in us, but we who are complete in Him. We are important in this Church, but we are not the primary structure; Christ Jesus is that strength.

The Scaffolding

In building our large structures it is necessary to erect scaffolding to support the workmen and materials. This is even more evident in masonry construction than in our high-rise buildings that are constructed by means of a crane in the center of the structure. So massive is the amount of scaffolding necessary in masonry construction that the building itself can hardly be seen. A casual observer might think that the building was being constructed with pipe stands held together with braces fastened with wing nuts, but this is not the structure; it is the scaffold. It surrounds the building, it supports the masons and tons of materials, and it makes work on the building possible, but it is temporary; it is not the building.

In building the Church, God has erected much scaffolding; so much, as a matter of fact, that few people actually see the Church that is under construction, but they can accurately describe the scaffolding. How aware we are of denominations, doctrines, ordinances, offices, rites, rituals, ceremonies, and commandments, but these are not the Church; they are scaffold. The moment we say "church" our mind envisions buildings, chancels, pulpits, pews, stained glass, pipe organs, robed choirs, vested clergy, carpeted aisles, and potted plants, but these are not the Church either; they are scaffold.

In constructing the real Church, God surrounds it with

scaffolding that is unreal, for the permanent Church uses temporary ministries as a platform for the workmen. While the eternal Church is invisible, the Church in our time dimension is very visible, but most of what is visible is little more than scaffolding. The pomp, program, and personalities of the visible Church are often part of the construction of the invisible Church, but when the building has been completed, all of this external scaffolding will be torn down and carried away. Only then will the glory of God's architecture be seen in its resplendent beauty. Then its style, lines, and shape will be seen without the distortion of scaffold and planks.

Today the world mocks the Church, calling it a subculture or minority group, but when the Church is complete and the outer scaffolding is removed, that Church will be seen as a Kingdom so forceful as to be indestructible in this world. Then the world, and many churchmen, will discover that the great joy of the local church is that it isn't local—it is but one of many stones in a much greater trans-local Church of the living God that encompasses the redeemed of all races, periods of history, and theological persuasions.

The true Church does not belong to the clergy; it belongs to God. It is not being built by men; God is building His Church. The Church has not been designed by constitutions and bylaws; its plans have been drawn by Almighty God Himself, and He is overseeing all stages of the construction. This magnificent, world-encompassing Church is not a structure for men to come into; it is a habitation for the triune God here on earth; and its duration is not measured in the span called time; it is eternal and shall endure throughout all eternity.

That Christ is its framework is indisputable, but that the

redeemed, justified, reconciled saints are the "living stones" that make up the rest of the building is equally incontestable, for Paul ends this chapter by saying, "In him you too are being built with all the rest into a spiritual dwelling for God" (Ephesians 2:22 NEB).

8

We Are Builded Together

Because our concept of a temple or church is that of a place where we are comfortably seated while a worship service is conducted, we tend to think of God's eternal Church as a place where saints gather for spiritual fellowship and feasting on Christ Jesus, but we are *not seated* in this holy temple—we *become* that temple. We "are all part of this building in which God himself lives by his Spirit" (Ephesians 2:22 PHILLIPS). The temple is the showplace of God. Renowned for its beauty, admired for its grandeur, and revered for its atmosphere, it is symbolic of the presence of God and synonymous with His habitation on earth.

We Are the Superstructure

In saying that we "are built upon the foundation of the apostles and prophets . . ." (Ephesians 2:20), the aorist form of the Greek word denotes the act of *being* built upon, and can be translated as "from the foundation" or "over the foundation," which would point to further building. In the Latin Vulgate Version of the Bible, used by the Roman Catholic church, the Latin word *superaedificate* is used. In English we have the noun *superstructure*—but no corre-

151

sponding verb—which basically signifies that which is being built over or upon. So Paul views the process as progressive, but, as of now, incomplete.

In the preceding chapter we concerned ourselves with the skeletal structure of the holy temple, but here we want to see the superstructure, or that which completes the building. As necessary as foundations, pillars, floors, and archways are, if that is all that remains standing, they are referred to as "ruins." While Christ is the structural support of the entire temple, the saints become the superstructure, or that which completes the building.

In speaking of our being "fitly framed together," Paul apparently compounded a word as an architectural metaphor, and it is used only here and in Ephesians 4:16, where the metonymy is the growth of a body rather than the building of a temple. His word implies a joining of living members, as in a plant, more than the joining of stones and timbers. It is not so much a picture of things sitting one on another as it is of separate items being shaped so as to sit within one another, not too unlike a mortise joint or the interlocking pieces of a jigsaw puzzle.

In modern architecture, once the skeletal structure has been framed, the rest of the building either hangs on it or butts against it, but in masonry construction the stones must interweave, overlap, and often be cut so as to sit inside one another. This is Paul's concept. We are so "fitly framed together" one with another and with Christ that we rest in Him, are interwoven with Him, and actually become an integral part of the structure for which He has formed the skeleton.

We Are Being Built Together

To this Paul adds the expression "ye also are builded together . . ." (Ephesians 2:22), using the Greek word *sunoikodomeisthe*, which A. T. Robertson, in his book *Word Pictures in the New Testament*, says is "present passive indicative (continuous process) of (a) common old verb *sunoikodomeō*, to build together with others or out of varied materials as here."

We are being built together with Christ, whom God has chosen to be the framework for the entire structure. We are skillfully being fitted into Him so that we take our place of utility much as a drawer fits into a desk or chest. But this special habitation of God can never merely be "just Jesus and me," as the songwriter would suggest, for we are not only being fitted into Christ Jesus but are being built up together with other believers. Furthermore, God's Church is constructed with materials beyond our own circle of friends or our doctrinal or denominational fellowships.

God is building His Church with little or no regard for man's designs or desires. There are not many churches or holy temples; there is only one. This Church of the living God is being constructed of materials over which we exercise no control; Christ chooses His own stones from the ruins of the fallen temple of humanity. Those materials that God chooses are cut and fitted together to construct that which the mind of God had conceived: a habitation of God among men.

Back in 1688 John Bunyan, best known for his *Pilgrim's Progress,* wrote a very lengthy poem about the building of the house of God. The first stanza reads:

The builder's God, materials his Elect,
His Son's the rock on which it is erect;
The Scripture is his rule, plummet, or line,
Which gives proportion to this house divine,
His working-tools his ordinances are,
By them he doth his stones and timber square,
Affection knit in love, the couplings are,
Good doctrine like to mortar doth cement
The whole together, schism to prevent;
His compass, his decree; his hand's the Spirit
By which he frames, what he means to inherit,
A holy temple, which shall far excel
That very place, where now the angels dwell.

Quite obviously the gift of the poet goes beyond the ability to turn a good phrase; he is blessed with brevity! Paul must have possessed some poetic gift to have expressed the truth in so few succinct words: "In whom ye also are builded together for an habitation of God through the Spirit." We are the materials, the Holy Spirit is the agent, Christ is the framework, and God will be its resident. What marvelous company the saints have been invited to keep. We who have become partakers of Christ are invited to become participants with Christ and to be positioned in Christ as part of the residence of God here on earth.

The Construction Is Continuous

That the building is not yet complete is obvious both by observation and by the very word Paul used—*sunoikodomeisthe*—which signifies a continuous process; the construction is still going on. This glorious temple will continue to increase and be more and more perfect until the final day of judgment. Even though the beginnings of the Church were glorious, its ending will be even more glorious. The early Church grew by multiplication, rather than by addition; should not we, then, expect that in the last days the Church will also know growth by multiplication? Since "better is the end of a thing than the beginning thereof . . ." (Ecclesiastes 7:8), we can watch in great expectation as God puts the finishing touches on this holy temple He has been constructing for many hundreds of years.

Paul was not the only apostle who visualized the temple of God's being constructed out of believers who have been joined together with Christ and with one another, for Peter wrote virtually the same thing. Interestingly enough, Peter used the same Greek word as Paul, without the prefix *sun,* when he speaks of our being "built up a spiritual house" (1 Peter 2:5). While it is highly improbable that these two men conferred about the subject, it does seem obvious that each was learning from the same Teacher, the Holy Spirit. Like Paul, Peter first reveals what Jesus Christ is to this spiritual house, and then he speaks of the part the Christians play in its construction.

"So come to him," Peter wrote, "our living Stone—the stone rejected by men but choice and precious in the sight of God. Come, and let yourselves be built, as living stones, into a spiritual temple; become a holy priesthood, to offer spiritual sacrifices acceptable to God through Jesus Christ" (1 Peter 2:4,5 NEB). In these brief words Peter tells us that what Christ is, we are; where Christ is, we are; and what He gives, we give.

What Christ Is, We Are

Peter's first delineation of Christ is as "our living Stone" (1 Peter 2:4), which may suggest that the Church is not built upon the philosophy, doctrine, ministry, teaching, or example of its founder; the Church is built upon the Founder Himself—the Lord Jesus Christ—who declared, "I am he that liveth, and was dead; and, behold, I am alive for evermore, Amen ..." (Revelation 1:18). It is this living Christ, not the memory of a Jesus who once lived, that has become the hope of the Church. This is the cardinal contrast between Christianity and other major religions of the world. Mohammed lived and died; Confucius lived and died; but Jesus Christ died and now lives! He alone is the living Stone.

Peter also calls this living Stone "a chief corner stone" in quoting from Isaiah 28:16. Then he quotes from the psalmist, "The stone which the builders refused is become the head stone of the corner" (Psalms 118:22). In *The Speaker's Bible,* Dr. James Hastings tells of a beautiful tradition that is handed down to us from the building of Solomon's temple concerning this stone that was rejected by the builders.

> Down from the mountains it was brought by the straining oxen, but no place could be found for it in the rising walls. After repeated attempts to dispose of it, it was rolled aside, where it was soon covered by moss and weeds. As the building neared completion a special stone was needed to knit together the two walls at the corner. This need reminded builders of the stone which had been rejected. The moss and weeds were brushed aside. The stone was carried to the place where it was needed, and though of peculiar shape it exactly fitted the place where it was wanted. Thus the stone that was rejected by the builders became the headstone of the corner.

What a picture of Christ: unwanted but needed; discovered and exalted.

No matter whether God places this living Stone in the foundation, the wall, or at the key position in the arch, He is very much alive and is involved with His Church. His life infuses all around Him, and He, the "living Stone," transforms us into "living stones." What He is, we become! We've already discovered that ours is not an inherent life, for we were hopelessly dead in sins, but Christ has conferred His life to us by "quickening us together with Christ" (Ephesians 2:5). Just as Paul ties the redeemed ones to their Redeemer in the temple construction, Peter says that "we are living stones"—stones that have been made alive through association with the living Stone. When Peter made his great confession of faith, Christ said, "Thou art Peter, and upon this rock I will build my church ..." (Matthew 16:18). Could Peter ever get this out of his mind? The Lord Himself had declared that the Church would be built upon the Rock, and Peter's very name means "rock." Although this little stone, this "piece of the rock," had denied the true Rock, Peter had been revitalized by a brief association with "that spiritual Rock ... and that Rock was Christ" (1 Corinthians 10:4), and from that day forward Peter was also "a living stone."

Similarly, we have received the imparted nature of Christ until what He is, we have become, but in much smaller quantity, of course. Master Mason that He is, God is not mixing stones in His temple; He desires the same quality of stone in the entire structure. To accomplish this, He must make us like His Son, Jesus, so that we can be joined together with Him in this holy temple, the Church.

An experienced stonemason can tell a living stone from a dead stone by the ring of his trowel when he strikes the stone. Not only will the trowel "sing," but the stone itself will vibrate. There is a massive visual presentation of the difference between living stone and dead stone at Stone Mountain in Atlanta, Georgia. There, over a period of many years, sculptors have carved into the face of the largest piece of exposed granite in all America an enormous statue of General Robert E. Lee astride his horse. At the base of this carving lies an impressive mound of granite that obviously is the residue of this work. Visitors are told that the workmen had to cut thirty feet into the face of this huge granite mountain before they could find live stone that would support the carving. The elements had destroyed the life and vitality of the stone to that depth, and they would not waste their efforts on dead stone.

Neither will God. He will not build Himself an eternal habitation out of materials that have already begun to decay. But He will, and does, reach into the dregs of human experience to pick up one in whom the workings of death are firm and settled and impart divine life to him, making him usable material for this holy temple.

Where He Is, We Are

Christ is in His Church. In John's vision he saw Christ standing in the midst of the candlesticks, which were defined as the local congregations of the invisible Church (*see* Revelation 1:12). Christ is not only in His Church as a resident, but He is in this Church as an integral part of its structure. Having been made alive by association with Him, we are invited to join Him as a part of the living Church. "So come to him," Peter wrote, "... and let yourselves be built, as living stones, into a spiritual temple ..." (1 Peter 2:4,5 NEB). It is an invitation far more than an imperative. The

Spirit solicits our participation in God's building program, not to be the builders but to be the building material.

We are invited to be "living stones," not baked bricks. Although by nature we may seem to be more clay and straw than polished marble, God has not chosen to build His temple out of our nature; He infuses His own holy nature into us. Man's religious system is generally constructed of brick, for the material is far more readily available to him, and he likes the uniformity. An experienced brick mason should be able to lay as many square feet of brick per hour as a stonemason can lay of stone in a full day. For those in a hurry, bricks are best. But God is not in a hurry, and He doesn't delight in uniformity. God is so creative that no two snowflakes are identical; neither are people all alike. Why, then, would we expect God to put His reconciled children into a brick mold and fashion us all alike? Instead, God makes us living stones and then cuts and fits us according to our utility to Him in His temple construction.

Cut and Fit for Placement

Laying stone can be compared to an immense vertical jigsaw puzzle in which you must cut the next piece rather than locate it. It is this cutting and fitting that is so time-consuming. The mason mentally measures the cavity in the wall that needs to be filled and then surveys his stone pile, seeking a piece that may be similar in shape and size to what is needed. That stone is either taken to the wall or a measurement from the wall is taken to the stone, and the stone is marked for cutting. When the stonecutter is certain that this is the correct stone, he takes it to the cutting box, which is merely a sandbox with a large piece of angle iron imbedded in the sand. Placing the stone over the protruding tip of this iron, exactly under the spot he wants to cut off, the stonecutter pulls sand around and under the stone so that it is completely supported by the sand, and then he places his chisel along the marked line on top and begins to gently tap the chisel with his hammer. Between each blow the chisel is moved a little along the line. Tap, tap, tap echoes across the building site as steel meets steel, and the chisel cuts into stone. Eventually the ring becomes a hollow thud, and the mason knows that the rock has broken. Lining up his chisel directly above the steel that is under the cut, he hits a final solid blow, and the rock breaks in a straight line across its face.

It may be necessary to make a second and occasionally a third cut before the stone fits the section of the wall for which it was chosen. This cut stone is then "faced" by chipping the sharp edges off with angle blows from the mason's hammer, and then it is placed into the section of the wall for which it has been fitted. Sometimes it is mortared in immediately; other times the mason will prefer to cut many stones and then cement them all into place at the same time. If the stone crumbles or breaks erratically during this process, it is set aside for use in a smaller cavity of the wall.

While there may be some living stones that have been fitted into the walls of God's spiritual house without having to be cut and trimmed to shape, most of us can identify with the hammer-and-chisel ministry of God's Holy Spirit. How well I remember some of my trips to the sandbox! It seemed that God was particularly anxious to square me up. I was misshapen and would not have bonded well with other living stones, so God kept cutting away those things in my life that were out of proportion with His plans for me. I made repeated trips to the wall for measurement, and then back to the cutting box I went. How well I knew the feel of the tap, tap, tap of the hammer as the chisel made a groove across an area of my life.

Perhaps the most painfully distressing part of God's sandbox is that He tends to cut off the most valuable part of our lives. God cut off and threw away the areas where I thought that I had the greatest strength and capability. He took my musical ministry away from me completely, for instance, and drastically changed my style of public ministry. It seemed that any area in which I had developed expertise, He chiseled off and threw on the scrap heap, while closely guarding and cutting into shape the areas that I considered to be the least developed or useful to God's kingdom. But I am not the stonemason; I am but the stone, and as such I have no control over what shall be used and what shall be refused. All the while I am in the sandbox, I am totally at the mercy of the Stonecutter. If He is skillful, I will be useful; if not, I will be wasted.

Placed Into Position

If we have not learned of the tender mercies of the Lord before He begins to fit us into His wall, we may develop a seriously negative attitude toward God. Because we are experiencing pain and loss, we might conceive of God as harsh and unloving. But God does not work according to our apparent emotional needs; He is building Himself a house, and we are being prepared to take our place in this structure. We are useless to Him as we are, so He reforms us through the action of His Spirit and His Word.

Not only do we not have a voice in what shape we will eventually become; we also have no say in where we will be placed in the wall. Our vote would probably be for a position in the front of the building, as close as possible to the front door, but the walls to the side and back of the building must be constructed, too. The lower portions of the walls, which will probably be unseen because of the shrubbery, must be built, and that will take hewn stone—living stone that has been cut to fit. Obviously, it is impossible for every stone to be placed so as to be easily visible.

Furthermore, we have no choice over with whom we will be bonded. How unwisely do we explain to the Lord that we want to be fitted in the wall alongside of, and resting on, those of exactly the same doctrinal persuasion as we. More likely than not God will place us in the wall with living stones with whom we have had little or no fellowship, and perhaps with some we have held as being a little suspect. When our pleas for a transfer are ignored, we begin to discover that God has done a work in their lives very similar to the work He has done in ours, and that we actually fit together very beautifully. God is, you know, a Master Mason.

Even after I got comfortable in having to rest upon living stones about whom I knew little or nothing, I became very uncomfortable with the stones God seemed to want to place around and over me. The brother He placed directly over me had a large "v" protrusion in his life, and as God placed him on me, he rocked back and forth precariously. When God picked him up, I sympathetically said, "Oh, brother, do I feel sorry for you! I know what God is going to do to you, for I've spent much time in that sandbox."

But, to my amazement, God set that stone aside and picked me up and carried me to the cutting box, where He proceeded to chisel a v-shaped groove in my back.

"God," I cried, "what are You doing to me? You spent

hours smoothing my back until it was square, straight and level."

"I'm merely adapting you to your brother," was the reply.

It was a long and painful process to cut a deep groove in me, but when I was returned to the wall, and my brother was placed on me again, we fit together like a hand in a glove. God didn't want two flat stones sitting one on the other; He chose to "fitly frame" us together so that the wall would have increased strength.

Cemented Together

God is not building a pyramid; He is building a temple, and the stones must be cemented together with mortar. God's bonding mortar is faith and love. These two are so blended together as to be reminiscent of the cement and lime that make up the bonding mortar in stone work. Everything that God does is tempered by love, and every area in which we cooperate with God is tempered with faith. Just as cement and lime must be blended together to get a working mortar, so faith and love need to be compounded together to firmly fix us in our position in God's temple.

We are told that faith works by love (*see* Galatians 5:6); that is, love is the channel through which faith functions, or love is the catalyst that produces a faith response. We are also told that "without faith it is impossible to please [God]" (Hebrews 11:6). It cannot be without signification that in the past decade there has been a fresh emphasis upon love and faith in the Church. God is mixing mortar for the completion of His temple. His living stones will cohere to one another through the working of faith and love when nothing else will cause them to stick together.

Since both faith and love have their source in the heavens,

we are not expected to produce them; we merely receive them, allow ourselves to be surrounded by them, and find ourselves firmly fixed in God's perfect will by their presence.

A Vision of This Holy Temple

The phone in my motel room rang rudely, jarring my thoughts from the theme I was writing at that moment. The call was from my brother Robert, who pastors a large church in Salem, Oregon, where my parents attended. "Judson," he said, "I don't want to unduly alarm you, but if you want to see Mother alive you had better catch the next plane to Salem. The doctor says that she cannot pull through this time."

I arranged with the conference director to be released from ministry immediately and was en route from the East Coast to the West Coast that very day. Arriving in Portland, I immediately rented a car and drove directly to my mother's house in Salem. She was both surprised and elated to see me, and although she was very weak, she said she had something very important to tell me.

It seems that she felt she had undergone an out-of-body experience, and she wanted me to judge whether what she had seen and heard was real or merely a hallucination. She said that sometime after her pacemaker had stopped functioning, or during the surgical implantation of a second instrument, she left her body in a sensation of rising. A person clothed in white met her, and they continued their ascent together. Above, and beyond her, was a glistening white object that completely captured her attention, for from it issued the most beautiful music she had ever heard. As they continued to rise, she was able to determine that this object was a large building, and as she got even closer, she could tell that it was a temple built of glistening white stone.

When she was closer still, her angelic attendant pointed out to her that each stone was made up of several individuals who were fitted together and shaped to join in the wall perfectly. Each person seemed to be winged, and it was the gentle flutter of these wings that gave the glistening effect to the light. She also said that the light seemed to come from within the temple by shining through these composite stones.

While she marveled at these translucent, glittering stones, her attention was directed to the cupola that formed the second and highest dome of this temple. The temple appeared to be complete except for two stones in the topmost section of this cupola. She watched while angels gathered individuals together, formed them into the final two stones, and lovingly placed them into position and gently held them there. The moment those final two stones were set in place the building came ablaze with light of a far greater intensity than before, and the music swelled into cascading crescendos as the worship within the temple seemed to flow out through the living stones and permeate the atmosphere for an incalculable distance around it.

Mother told me in her weak voice that never in all of her Christian experience had she heard worship that would compare with what she heard coming from that beautiful temple. Her attention was again directed to the angels who were holding the final two stones in place. Slowly they removed their hands to see if the stones were firmly set in their places, but almost immediately these two stones floated out of place and began to come apart. Immediately the worship ceased, the music diminished, and the light dimmed noticeably. Tenderly the angels regathered the individuals, compacted them into stones again, and replaced them in the dome once more. Again the music swelled, the light intensified, and the worship poured forth from within the temple.

For quite a season the angels held these stones in place, but when they removed their hands, the stones again withdrew from their positions and began to come apart.

"I'm not sure what all this means," Mother told me through her great weakness, "but I felt that it was important that I tell it to you."

"Mother," I told her, "what you have just told me is real. God has allowed you to see and experience what I have been preaching about for several years. God's temple is nearly complete. The light of God's glory and the beauty of worship is about to be heard throughout all of the earth. But the final stones are resistive to the perfect will of God. Until they learn to not only get together but to stay together, we will experience the light and sound of God's presence only as the angels hold them in place."

It probably is not my place to try to define these final two stones, but if we are as close to the end of time as we think we are, they surely must represent the workings of God in our generation. How wonderfully have we been drawn and molded together in the great conventions of the past twenty years. Under the guiding hand of the Holy Spirit we have been placed in position in God's temple, and light, song, and worship have filled the air. But it seems that when the convention is over, we go our separate ways with our independent spirits, and the glorious worship in the temple ceases. How God yearns for us to learn what others before us have learned so completely: Only when we stay together as God has placed us will anything of eternal value transpire in our generation. Worship does not take place during the construction of the temple, but after its completion.

A Dwelling Place for God

Paul concludes his illustration with the words, "You are all part of this building in which God himself lives by his Spirit" (Ephesians 2:22 PHILLIPS). We are that temple; God is its inhabitant. We give it particular structural character, and He gives it purpose for existence. The entire structure is unto the praise of His glory; it is for His utilization, and it is His habitation among men.

It is not accidental that Paul uses the Greek word *naos* for "temple" rather than *hieron,* for while *hieron* describes the whole of the temple precincts, *naos* is the word used for the inner shrine—that portion of the temple where God resided. In the tabernacle of witness in the wilderness this was called "the Holy of Holies" and was so sacred that no man, unbidden, dared to enter it. It was the place on which the glory of God descended, the place of His presence. When Christ came He became the tabernacle among men, the place where God's glory resided and where the divine presence could be met. But both of these tabernacles are gone from the earth now. In their place is something far more glorious, for now God seeks as His habitation the lives of men who will allow Him to enter by His Spirit.

God is building a temple, a *naos*—a divine residence— and we are part of that structure. "Know ye not that ye are the temple of God, and that the Spirit of God dwelleth in you?" Paul asks (1 Corinthians 3:16), and "What? know ye not that your body is the temple of the Holy Ghost which is in you, which ye have of God, and ye are not your own? For ye are bought with a price: therefore glorify God in your body, and in your spirit, which are God's" (1 Corinthians 6:19,20).

In his commentary on the Bible, Adam Clarke makes the following observation about the Church:

The Church of God is very properly said to be a most noble and wonderful work, and truly worthy of God himself.

There is nothing, says one, so *august* as this Church, seeing it is the *temple of God.*

Nothing so worthy of *reverence,* seeing God *dwells* in it.

Nothing so *ancient,* since the *patriarchs* and *prophets* laboured in building it.

Nothing so *solid,* since *Jesus Christ* is the *foundation* of it.

Nothing more closely *united* and *indivisible,* since he is the *corner stone.*

Nothing so *lofty,* since it reaches as high as *heaven,* and to the *bosom of God* himself.

Nothing so *regular* and *well proportioned,* since the *Holy Spirit* is the *architect.*

Nothing more *beautiful,* or *adorned* with greater *variety,* since it consists of *Jews* and *Gentiles,* of every *age, country, sex,* and *condition:* the mightiest *potentates,* the most renowned *lawgivers,* the most profound *philosophers,* the most eminent *scholars,* besides all of those *of whom the world was not worthy,* have formed a part of this building.

Nothing more *spacious,* since it is spread over the whole earth, and takes in all who have washed their robes, and made them white in the blood of the Lamb.

Nothing so *inviolable,* since it is consecrated to Jehovah.

Nothing so *Divine,* since it is a *living* building, *animated* and *inhabited* by the *Holy Ghost.*

It is the *place* in which God does his marvellous works; the *theatre* of his justice, mercy, goodness, and truth; where he is to be sought, where he is to be *found* and in which alone he is to be *retained.*

This is God's temple, His house, His Church that forms His home here among men, and we, when we are willing to get together and stay together, form this habitation. We form it not only as living stones, but as a living organism, for the Temple that becomes the habitation of God is also called the Body of Christ.

9

We Are Joined Together

When Paul said that "the building ... groweth unto an holy temple in the Lord" (Ephesians 2:21), he not only alluded to the continuous construction or the incomplete state of the present construction, but he suggested that there is a life within the materials that tends to enlarge and grow. We are not totally passive in the erection of this temple, for we are "living stones." Some of the work is done in us, some of it is done for us, and some of it is done by us. Even when Paul affirmed that "we are labourers together with God" he added, "... Ye are God's husbandry, ye are God's building," thereby combining inanimate construction with animate growth (1 Corinthians 3:9).

We've already noted that when writing about the construction of God's holy temple, Paul double-compounded a Greek word which he used as an architectural metaphor, and which we have translated as "fitly framed together." He used this word again in referring to the Body of Christ when he wrote, "From whom the whole body *fitly joined together*" (Ephesians 4:16, italics added). The double use of this tailor-made word is indicative that Paul is sharing the same concept, but from two distinctly different views of the action—one from without, the other from within.

In speaking of the Body being *sunarmologoumenon* ("fitly

framed together"), Paul writes, ". . . We must grow up in
every way to Christ, who is the head. Under his control all
the different parts of the body fit together, and the whole
body is held together by every joint with which it is provided. So when each separate part works as it should, the
whole body grows and builds itself up through love" (Ephesians 4:15,16 TEV).

We Are the Body of Christ

Several times Paul merges the terms "Church" and
"Body" in saying, ". . . the church, which is his body . . ."
(Ephesians 1:22,23); ". . . Christ is the head of the body, the
church . . ." (Colossians 1:18); ". . . for his body's sake,
which is the church" (Colossians 1:24); and "now ye [the
church] are the body of Christ . . ." (1 Corinthians 12:27). It
is a serious violation of the laws of hermeneutics to try to
make two separate groups out of these two terms, for they
are one and the same company of people merely seen or
mentioned under different figures of speech. As surely as we
are the Church of God, we are also the Body of Christ on
this earth. I've already mentioned that through Mary at
Bethlehem God gave Jesus a body that could die, and out of
the tomb God gave Him a body that could live, but it is
through the Church that God provides His Son a Body that
can function here on the earth.

As the functioning Body of Christ on the earth, the
Church becomes His hands and feet to do His bidding, His
heart to do His feeling, and His corporeal form to be extended to a lost and dying world. The only God that the
world will ever see is Christ's Body, the Church, for we are
the visible manifestation of the Godhead here on the earth.
If the glory of God is ever to be seen, it must be seen in

Christ's Body, and if the strength of God is ever demonstrated, it must be demonstrated in the Body of Christ. If the Word of God is to be heard in the countries of this world, it must be through the Body of Christ, for without this Body, Christ is but an invisible spirit to the natural man.

It is obvious that as the living Body of Christ we are not an organization but an organism. This means, then, that we will not be competitive but completive—we will not strive to become bigger and better than the other, but we will seek to complete the other members of the Body. A living Body is animated, not actuated. We are not mechanical robots controlled and actuated by motors and computers; we are living members of a larger unit, the Body of Christ, and it is a common life, not a common experience, that holds us together.

Since this Body is a living individual composed of mutually dependent parts and is animated by a common life, it becomes apparent that there is nothing we can do of our natural selves to become members in the Body of Christ. We cannot join it; we must be birthed into it by action of the Holy Spirit of God, for Paul said, "For by one Spirit are we all baptized into one body . . ." (1 Corinthians 12:13).

In his recent book *The Eternal Church,* Dr. Bill Hamon writes:

The only way a lower realm of life can be lifted up to the realm of a higher life is for it to be taken up and transformed into that higher realm of life. The lower realm of life has to *die and forsake its way* of life. The following analogy will illustrate this truth.

Minerals can be taken up and transformed into plant life.

Plants can be taken up and transformed into animal life.

Animal flesh can be taken up and transformed into human life.

Human life can be taken up and transformed into Christ's life.

Controlled Together

The first thing Paul tells us about this Body is that Christ "... is the head" (Ephesians 4:15). While this should be self-evident, the way we try to function here on earth indicates that far too frequently some human individual thinks that he is the head of the Church, Christ's Body. It goes without saying that any two-headed organism is a monster or a freak, and Christ's Body is neither of these.

The reality of one head makes this greatly diversified Body of Christ manageable and functional, for the several parts of the body all get their signals and orders from the same source: Christ. It is this central control that maintains unity in this heterogeneous unit called the Church and the Body of Christ. The Head commands, and the Body conforms. Christian unity becomes vital when a common life source animates all of the organs of the Body and a common head actuates it.

In speaking of the need and nature of unity in the Church, *The Wesleyan Bible Commentary* says.

Unity, but not uniformity, is God's plan and pattern for His people and church. ... It is a spiritual principle that unity and consequent peace are attained through the ignoring of unessential differences, just as it is a mathematical principle that averages are reached through the ignoring or harmonizing of differences. God knows and treats His children as individuals, or as the author of Hebrews puts it, "God dealeth with you as with sons" (Hebrews 12:7), thus indicating the fact that God recognizes and allows individual differences. Likewise group differences in denominations, church polity, culture, interests, occupations, and even doctrinal or religious emphases are not in themselves necessarily divisions in the body of Christ, nor do they necessarily prevent the unity of the Church. They may but represent a wholesome and enriching variety in the spiritual unity of the Church Universal. God created a highly diversified natural world that is nevertheless a cosmos or a universe.

While there is no way that the Body of Christ can have uniformity, it is equally difficult for this Body to be without unity as long as it is harmoniously related to the one Head, Christ Jesus, who is called "the saviour of the body" (Ephesians 5:23). It is this commonality of control which gives unity to the Church.

Fitted Together

That we are unified but diversified seems to be a difficult concept for some religionists to accept, for unless an individual is exactly like them, they refuse to acknowledge that he is also a member of the Body of Christ. But Paul says, "Under his control all the different parts of the body fit together..." (Ephesians 4:16 TEV). Christ is the spiritual "DNA factor" for His Body, for just as the DNA factor in the individual cells of our human body determined how the parts of our body came together, to what size each would grow, which parts would have hair and which would be smooth, and so forth, Christ determines the placement and all related factors for the individual parts of His Body, the Church.

After declaring that "by one Spirit are we all baptized into one body ..." Paul adds, "For the body is not one member, but many" (1 Corinthians 12:13,14) and goes on to speak of individual parts of the body and the need for them to fit.

The obviousness of Paul's illustration prevents me from going into detail, for each of us lives in a body made up of many parts, and we have learned to honor each member of that body even though its function may be very different from that of other parts. Although we instinctively know and accept this, we still have difficulty transferring this elementary illustration to the spiritual Body of Christ, for in the Church, diversity is still suspect and uniformity is a standard definition of unity.

In the goodness of God we have not only been set in the Body; we fit together in this Body! "All the different parts of the body fit together." God has blended these parts together in one symmetrically beautiful and functionally useful unit called the Body of Christ. We don't have to work our way in as parasites; we have been set in, and we fit perfectly. While it is true that we are varied in nature, form, and operation and are helplessly dependent upon one another, we have been joined together in a growth process by an action beyond ourselves. It is not mechanical; it is animate. It is not by self-determination; it is by divine decree.

Unity means neither uniformity nor equality. Some Christians talk much about equality in ministry and office. Organizationally they might force the point, but organically it is a hopeless argument, for how can a foot and a hand be considered equal? Is a heart equal to a finger? All are important, of course, but because of the great difference in their functions, there is no basis for comparison. It is like trying to compare apples and bananas where, beyond each being classified as a fruit, there is no commonality between them. It is overdue for the members of the Body of Christ to stop trying to be equal and to begin functioning in a manner consistent with their placement in the Body, for the Bible declares, "But now hath God set the members every one of them in the body, as it hath pleased him" (1 Corinthians 12:18). If, indeed, God has fitted us together, let's accept our placement and position in the Body regardless of where it may be and function according to the unction we have received from the Spirit of God.

When Paul described the Church with the simile of a temple, we pictured ourselves being fitted together by the action of a stonemason who cut us to match an opening in the wall, but now Paul speaks of our being individual members in the Body of Christ. This fitting is far more intricate and intimate, for we do not merely rest one upon another, held together with cement and mortar, but we actually become a living part of one another in a most vital and viable way. So closely related do we become that when one member suffers, all members are affected, and, similarly, pleasure to one portion of the Body brings joy and satisfaction to the entire Body. We are not only essentially united with Christ, the Head of the Body; we are especially united with the many members who make up the Body of Christ on the earth.

Held Together

Being placed together is done by an outside force— God—but being held together requires an action within the Body itself. Paul said, ". . . And the whole body is held together by every joint with which it is provided" (Ephesians 4:16 TEV). Qualified students of the Greek language admit that there is some ambiguity in this portion of the verse because of the multiple uses the words have in classical Greek, but most of them agree that our translators have remained faithful to the intent of Paul without doing violence to the actual vocabulary he used.

The Rev. Francis Foulkes, the principal of Vining Christian Leadership Centre in Akure, Nigeria, writes in the *Tyndale New Testament Commentary:*

> The word translated joint (*haphē*) has many meanings. Basically it means a "touch," and so can mean "contact," "point of contact," or "grip," and these meanings have led commentators to a variety of interpretations. Both the context and the medical usage of the word for a "joint" of the body justify the AV rendering, and most English translations follow this. The Greek then would literally be taken "through every joint of the supply," and *that which every joint supplieth* [KJ] is hardly possible as a translation. Rather it is through every joint with which the body is equipped—"every constituent joint" (NEB)—that growth and true functioning is possible. In other words, the body depends for its growth and its work on the Lord's direction, on His provision for the whole (compare verses 11,12) and on His arrangements for the inter-relation of the members as well.

There is another verse in Paul's letters that is a close parallel to this one; in it Paul states, "Under Christ's control the whole body is nourished and held together by its joints and ligaments, and grows as God wants it to grow" (Colossians 2:19 TEV). Whatever philological problem these verses may present, Paul's illustration demands an understanding that the Body of Christ is held together by the "joints," "ligaments," "sinews," and "muscles" (as various translators express it) that God has put into this Body.

In *The Moffatt New Testament Commentary,* Dr. E. F. Scott says:

> The thought and language are adopted from Colossians 2:19, and have to be explained in the same manner. Paul looks at the body from the point of view of ancient medical science. It was believed that the cohesion of the body was due to two factors: (a) to the contact of one part with another; (b) to the nerves and tissues which bind all the different parts together like cords. These ligaments not only unify the body, but serve as the channels by which it receives its nourishment. The servants of Christ, on whom he bestowed the various spiritual gifts, are conceived as thus binding the Church together and conveying to every part of it the vitality they have derived from the head. Thus united and sustained, *welded together and compacted,* the Church continues to grow "according to the working in measure of each several part." Every element of the body, however insignificant, has something to contribute towards the well-being of the whole.

Inasmuch as the concept of a growing Body is not introduced in Ephesians until Paul has described the gifted individuals who have been set in the Church "for the edifying of the body of Christ" (Ephesians 4:12), it is likely that they were viewed by Paul as part of the connecting sinews and ligaments in the Body. Wherever God's gifted officers are rejected, the Body of Christ loses cohesion and suffers dislocation or even dismemberment. The Body has a common

life, but it also needs a common bond, and apostles, prophets, evangelists, pastors, and teachers are all a part of that
bond.

But they are only a part; they do not form the whole.
Every joint with which the Body is provided helps to hold
Christ's Body together, whether we conceive of it as doctrine, practice, officers, interrelationship of the members, or
the flow of the Holy Spirit from one member to another.
Whatever the means or channel, all strength for this Body
comes from its Head, Jesus Christ. Since the strongest joints
disintegrate when life ceases to flow, what is needed in this
Body are joints, made alive by Christ, who are willing to
hold tightly with other portions of the Body; then that whole
Body will be able to function together in strength.

Working Together

The obvious goal of having a Body for Christ on the earth
is so that it can function on His behalf. This, of course, demands that the Body function as it was designed to function,
and that is exactly what Paul says: "... So when each separate part works as it should ..." (Ephesians 4:16 TEV). The
Body functions properly when the individual parts function
properly, but inactivity by a few parts may very well inca-
pacitate the other parts. When a congregation of believers
sits back waiting for their staff of pastors, teachers, prophets,
and musicians to perform on their behalf, the true Body of
Christ suffers, for there is only so much substituting that can
be done for the individual parts of the Body. The health and
utility of this Body demand consistent activity by every individual member of that Body.

The Church, or at least the local congregation that forms

a part of that Church, has been likened to a professional football game where there are eleven overworked and exhausted specialists and thousands of underexercised spectators. But God never refers to His Church as a spectator sport; He calls it a Body. Every part of this Body learns to function harmoniously, contributing to the overall good and productivity of the entire Body. Even the worship of this Body is a united activity, for Paul wrote, "At all your meetings, let everyone be ready with a psalm or a sermon or a revelation, or ready to use his gift of tongues or to give an interpretation; but it must always be for the common good" (1 Corinthians 14:26 JERUSALEM).

Some would argue that such liberty granted to individual members of the Body of Christ would produce bedlam in our massive public worship services, but they may be overlooking two prepositions Paul used in describing the interrelationship of the Body to its Head. First, he says that we "grow up *into* ... the head, even Christ; *from* whom the whole body ..." (Ephesians 4:15,16, italics added). There is an "into Him" and a "from Him," which speak of a concentrative energy flowing toward the Head and a diffusive energy spreading from the Head. Our human body has two sets of nerves. By the one set the brain, the thinking, planning, originating authority for the body, transmits its orders to the various members of the body. The order is received and the muscle contracts; the joint is moved; and the hand holds, or the foot walks. By the other set of nerves the reverse process flows, for the grasp that presses the hand, the rays that strike the eye, the pulsations that beat on the ear, are all transmitted to the brain, and the corresponding sensation is produced.

Such is the relation of Christ to the Church. Each member functions at His guidance, and each member transmits signals back to Christ, who feels sympathetically and compassionately with His Body here on earth. When members of this Body fail to function, the Body suffers inactivity, and the Head in turn suffers the loss of feedback signals that help determine further indications or signals to action, but when "each separate part works as it should," as Today's English Version puts it, the Body responds to the signals from the Head, and the Head receives necessary signals from that Body.

Growing Together

When this proper interrelationship functions, Paul says that "the whole body grows" (Ephesians 4:16 TEV). That growth is a primary law of the kingdom of God is well-known, for God rarely starts with a finished product; He prefers to plant a seed and let it grow. Just as the human body begins as an embryo in the womb and grows through the stages of birth, babyhood, childhood, and into adulthood, so the Body of Christ is given the inherent life of the Spirit of God, and it, too, is expected to grow. This growth is not so much the result of conscious activity on the part of the Body as it is a response by that Body to the life forces that have been implanted within it.

This growth of the Body is the fundamental theme of this fourth chapter of Ephesians, and Paul uses a variety of expressions to impress upon us that God's goal is that His Body on earth mature from childhood to manhood. Paul says that the gifted individuals whom Christ gave to His Church were "for the *perfecting* of the saints . . . for the *edi-*

fying of the body of Christ" (v. 12) and that their ministry
would continue until "we all come ... unto a *perfect man,*
unto the measure of the *stature of the fulness of Christ*" (v.
13). He says that we should ". . . be no more *children* . . ." (v.
14) but should ". . . *grow up* into him in all things, which is
the head, even Christ" (v. 15) (all italics added). God's message to the Church here at the end of the twentieth century
is GROW UP.

In *Calvin's Commentaries* John Calvin says:

> . . . No increase is advantageous, which does not bear a just
> proportion to the whole body. That man is mistaken who
> desires his own separate growth. If a leg or arm should
> grown to a prodigious size, or the mouth be more fully dis-
> tended, would the undue enlargement of those parts be
> otherwise than injurious to the whole frame? In like man-
> ner, if we wish to be considered members of Christ, let no
> man be anything for himself, but let us all be whatever we
> are for the benefit of each other. This is accomplished by
> love; and where it does not reign, there is no "edification,"
> but an absolute scattering of the church.

While growth may be painful, only sickness or disease can
prevent it in either the natural body or the spiritual Body of
Christ. All too frequently organized religion that boasts of
being "the Body of Christ" seems to resist every enlarged
concept, truth, and practice that the Holy Spirit brings to the
believers, but the true Church grows in spite of the com-
plaints and resistance of men. Look at the progress of doctrine throughout the history of the Church. Every new truth
inspired fresh inquisitions and martyrdoms, and yet the
Body of Christ silently grew anyway. The same is true of the

varied experiences that God has brought to His Church here on earth. While men have resisted them and called them "unscriptural," the true Body absorbed them and grew as the result of them. As long as there is spiritual health, there will be growth and development, but when we stop growing we actually start to die.

Peter, who visualized the Church as a spiritual house, also saw it as a living organism, for he wrote, "As newborn babes, desire the sincere milk of the word, that ye may grow thereby" (1 Peter 2:2), and he concluded his epistles with the injunction, "But grow in grace, and in the knowledge of our Lord and Saviour Jesus Christ . . ." (2 Peter 3:18). The milk of the Word and the flow of God's grace are seen as contributing agents for the growth of the Body. If individual members lack the Word and God's grace, they will be stunted, and if the whole Body of Christ be deprived of these two fundamentals, it, too, will be dwarfed. Growth demands innate life supplemented by a nutritious food supply. God is the source of both.

Loving Together

While inner life and an outer food supply may form the prime factors for growth, there is an almost equal need for TLC (tender loving care). The child that is held, fondled, and lovingly touched will mature far more rapidly and healthfully than the child who is deprived of loving emotional input. Love is not a luxury; it is a necessity. A person may exist without love, but none really lives without it. Many a person who has lost his way emotionally, mentally, and sometimes even physically has been restored to health and stability with nothing more than genuine, sincere love.

Is this not what John the Beloved was teaching when he wrote, "Behold, what manner of love the Father hath bestowed upon us, that we should be called the sons of God. . . . Beloved, now are we the sons of God, and it doth not yet appear what we shall be: but we know that, when he shall appear, we shall be like him; for we shall see him as he is" (1 John 3:1,2). God's love now declares us to be "sons"—Greek *teknon,* "children." The continued exposure to that love assures us such growth that when we see Christ we shall be like Him. We were born of love, have been nurtured in love, and shall mature in the love of God.

James Hastings observes in *The Speaker's Bible* that "the world covets the larger grain; Christ taught us to covet the larger heart." If mere knowledge would fully mature the Body of Christ, then certainly the churches of America should be full-grown, for no generation of Christians has had such a proliferation of Bible translations, gospel radio and television broadcasts, books, tapes, conventions, crusades, Christian magazines, and so forth. No nation has ever had more churches or greater liberty to practice religion than this one. Still, for all of this great wealth of spiritual truth that is available to us, the Church in America doesn't seem to have matured beyond the Church in some of the Third World nations.

Since it is love, and not knowledge, that builds up the Church, Paul assures us that ". . . when each separate part works as it should, the whole body grows and *builds itself up through love*" (Ephesians 4:16 TEV, italics added). The combined love from outside the Body (God's love) and inside that Body (saints' love) contributes to the growth and maturity of the entire Body of Christ. It is not merely Christ loving the Church, but the Church loving the Church, that enhances growth. While the organized church seeks to promote growth through welfare, child care, parking, and preaching, the Church of the living God, which is Christ's Body, induces growth through its several members ministering one to another in love.

When the letter was written to the Hebrews, the Spirit challenged them with "and let us consider one another to provoke unto love and good works" (Hebrews 10:24). The Amplified Bible translates this, "And let us consider and give attentive, continuous care to watching over one another, studying how we may stir up, (stimulate and incite) to love, and helpful deeds and noble activities."

In our earthly bodies it is amazing how carefully one member protects another from harm or danger, and how one member grooms, cleans, or strokes another. Should not such care be the standard behavior in the Body of Christ? We are challenged both to love one another and to provoke one another unto love. Each is a scriptural command. The Greek word we have translated "to provoke" is *paroxysmos,* which denotes a stimulation, and is the root for our English word *paroxysm,* meaning "a sudden attack, a sudden violent emotion, a convulsion or a fit." The members of Christ's Body should provoke a sudden violent emotion of love in other members of that Body. We owe it to one another to strengthen zeal, to inflame affection, and to kindle each other to a flame of love that is beyond mere sentiment or natural affection but is a holy principle of action, for where Christian love ceases, all of hell's activity begins. Satan works more against love than against any other Christian virtue, while Christ works more through love than through any other Christian attribute, since "...God *is* love" (1 John 4:8, italics added).

Because love is part of the essential nature of God Himself, and since the Church is also viewed as the Body of Christ—an extension of God here on the earth—we should expect that the one outstanding characteristic of the Church would be love. This is exactly what Christ taught when He said, "By this shall all men know that ye are my disciples, if ye have love one to another" (John 13:35). It is not love *for* but love *to*—love that is expressed or released to each other.

Where love in the Body fails, disunity prevails, and disunity in the members produces deformity in the Body. A dangerous condition that is occasionally observed is when members of the Body will love only similar members, and will withdraw from dissimilar members. Where this prevails, we end up with all hands in one place; all torsos in another; all legs in one area; and all feet in still another group. This may form a magnificent spare-parts bank, but it cannot form a living Body. What God's Body needs to learn is how to expressively love every segment of itself without qualification, reservation, or hesitation. It is Christ's Body; we are individual members of it; so it is worthy of being loved.

When this is done, unity prevails! Getting us together is not an artificial program but an animate production whereby the commonality of life produces a consciousness of interdependence that is connotative of love.

Christ has drawn us together by His cross, His life, His resurrection, His ascension, His Temple construction, and His Headship of the Body here on earth. We have not been asked to produce togetherness, merely to recognize it and to be a participant in it, "that their hearts might be comforted,

being knit together in love, and unto all riches of the full as-
surance of understanding, to the acknowledgement of the
mystery of God, and of the Father, and of Christ; In whom
are hid all the treasures of wisdom and knowledge" (Colossians 2:2,3).